Advance Praise for Amy James's Knowledge Esse

"Knowledge Essentials is a remarkable series that will benefit children of all abilities and learning styles. Amy James has taken a close look at curriculum standards and testing around the country and developed simple and creative activities that support what's being taught at each grade level, while remaining sensitiv_____ates and in different ways. I h_____ to make a difference in their_____

—_____ arn Differently
_____ Wonder of Boys

"Finally, a book ab_____ ho knows her stuff! I can (an_____ es to the ever-growing number c_____ they can help their children succ_____

—_____ ngerous Minds
_____ n of Education

"Having examined state standards nationwide, Amy James has created innovative and unique games and exercises to help children absorb what they *have* to learn, in ways that will help them *want* to learn. Individualized to the child's own learning style, this is a must-have series for parents who want to maximize their child's ability to succeed in and out of the classroom."

—Myrna B. Shure, Ph.D., author of *Thinking Parent, Thinking Child*

"The books in Amy James's timely and unique Knowledge Essentials series give parents a clear idea of what their children are learning and provide the tools they need to help their children live up to their full academic potential. This is must reading for any parent with a school-age child."

—Michele Borba, Ed.D., author of *Nobody Likes Me, Everybody Hates Me* and *No More Misbehavin'*

KNOWLEDGE
ESSENTIALS™

THIRD GRADE
SUCCESS

Everything You Need to Know
to Help Your Child Learn

AMY JAMES

JOSSEY-BASS
A Wiley Imprint
www.josseybass.com

To my dad, E. W. James

Published by Jossey-Bass
A Wiley Imprint
989 Market Street, San Francisco, CA 94103-1741

Design and composition by Navta Associates, Inc.

Jossey-Bass books and products are available through most bookstores. To contact Jossey-Bass directly call our Customer Care Department within the U.S. at 800-956-7739, outside the U.S. at 317-572-3986, or fax 317-572-4002.

Jossey-Bass also publishes its books in a variety of electronic formats. Some content that appears in print may not be available in electronic books.

Library of Congress Cataloging-in-Publication Data:

James, Amy, date.
   Third grade success : everything you need to know to help your child learn / Amy James.
      p. cm.
   Includes bibliographical references and index.
   ISBN-13 978-0-471-46821-9 (pbk.)
   ISBN-10 0-471-46821-5 (pbk.)
  1. Third grade (Education) 2. Third grade (Education)—Curricula—United States.
3. Education, Elementary—Parent participation. I. Title.
   LB15713rd .J36 2005
   372.24'1—dc22   2004031045

Printed in the United States of America

FIRST EDITION

PB Printing 10 9 8 7 6 5 4 3 2 1

CONTENTS

ACKNOWLEDGMENTS

I would like to thank the following people for advising me on this book:

My mother, Cindy King, is a retired early childhood and reading specialist who taught kindergarten and first grade for thirty years. She assisted in establishing the transition program at her school district for children who are developmentally young.

My father, E. W. James, was an elementary school principal and elementary school teacher for fifteen years. He led the school district's efforts to serve children with special needs.

Gloria Hamlin, my supervising administrator during my teaching years, retired from Norman Public School after spending twenty-two years teaching math and eleven years as a middle school administrator. She directed the math, science, and technology departments.

Elizabeth Hecox is in her sixteenth year of teaching at Kennedy Elementary School in Norman, Oklahoma. She is an incredible classroom teacher, and the book is better because of her work with me on it.

Kim Lindsay is in her twelfth year of teaching elementary school in Dallas Public Schools and in Norman Public Schools. She was elected teacher of the year at Kennedy Elementary School for 2001–2002.

Holly Sharp taught English language arts for thirty years in five states and served as department chair for twelve years. She has written curriculum for Norman Public Schools and is an advisory board member for both the University of Oklahoma and Norman Public Schools.

The employees of Six Things, Inc., are a group of more than twenty current and former teachers who provide invaluable assistance on a daily basis. Anytime I needed help in any subject area, for any grade, their enormously good brains were at my disposal. This book series would not be possible without their assistance, and I am eternally grateful to them for their help.

Introduction

Third grade probably brings back fond memories of being carefree on the playground, memorizing multiplication tables, and moving up the food chain from Brownie (or Cub Scout) to Girl (or Boy) Scout. Not so fast! Third grade is a whole new ball game where you have to prove you can read, write, and do math before the doors of fourth grade open. The name of the game is testing, and it is the only way to move from grade to grade from here on out.

You may be asking these questions: Is there a place for me in my child's education? Is a teaching certificate a prerequisite for helping with homework? What do you mean my child has to pass a test to advance to the next grade? Where is the closest boarding school?

Relax, calm down, and step away from the flash cards. Passing third grade isn't the hardest thing you are ever going to help your child do. You can handle it, and this book can help. The key isn't in drill and kill (also known as skill and drill) types of practice-until-you-memorize-it activities. Oh sure, there is some of that—particularly when it comes to memorizing the fifty states or the multiplication tables—but the key really lies in awareness of the third grade learning expectations of your state and your school, and encouraging your child to achieve them by making small differences in your home learning environment.

Life at home matters. An academically progressive home life is the key to effectively tracking your child's development as well as providing the opportunity to successfully apply knowledge. Creating the environment is about creating the opportunity to learn. The point is to bring the level of content and conversation in your daily life to the level that is in your child's school life. Home, your child's first learning environment, is the primary testing ground for new knowledge and skills.

Getting the Most from This Book

This book is a guide to creating an exceptional learning environment in your home. It contains curricula and skills unique to third grade presented in a way that makes it easy to put what you learn into practice immediately. This book serves as a tool to help solve the mystery behind creating a supportive, learning-rich environment in your home that fosters a thinking child's development while enriching his or her curricula. It contains dozens of mini–lesson plans that contain easy-to-use activities designed to help your child meet your state's learning requirements. An environmental learning section in each chapter tells you how to identify learning opportunities in the everyday world.

Chapters 2 through 4 give you some child development information to get you started. Teaching is about knowing the subject area you teach, but moreover it is about knowing the abilities of the students you teach. As a parent you can easily see the milestones your child reaches at an early age (crawling, walking, talking, etc.), but milestones are not always apparent in your six- to nine-year-old. These chapters explain the child development processes that take place during third grade, including what thinking milestones your child's brain is capable of and will reach in normal development during this time. In order for you to teach effectively, you will need to account for these developmental milestones in all topics and skills that you introduce.

Teaching is also about recognizing how different people learn and tailoring the way you teach to suit them. You will find out how to recognize different learning styles in chapter 3, which will help you implement the learning activities in the rest of the book.

Chapters 5 through 11 provide general subject area information for the third grade curriculum. The curriculum discussed in this book was chosen by reviewing all fifty of the state learning standards, the National Subject Area Association learning standards, the core curriculum materials that many school districts use, and supplemental education products. While there are some discrepancies in curricula from region to region, they are few and far between. Chances are that even if you aren't able to use all of the topical subject area units (such as social studies and science), you will be able to use most of them. Reading, writing, and math are skill-based subjects, particularly in third grade, and those skills are chosen according to specific child developmental indicators. It is likely that you will be able to use all of the information in those chapters. Each chapter provides learning activities that you can do at home with your child.

The focus of chapter 12 is understanding the social environment in third grade, including how your child interacts with peers and his or her social needs. Chapter 13 discusses how your child will demonstrate that he or she is prepared for fourth grade. The appendixes provide information on products that meet certain third grade learning needs.

You won't read this book from cover to cover while lounging on the beach. Hopefully it will be a raggedy, dog-eared, marked-up book that has been thumbed through, spilled on, and referred to throughout the school year. Here are some tips on using this book:

Do

- Use this book as a reference guide throughout your child's third grade year.

- Model activities and approaches after the information you find in this book when creating your own supplemental learning activities.

- Modify the information to meet your needs and your child's needs.

Don't

- Complete the activities in this book from beginning to end. Instead, mix and match them appropriately to the curriculum and/or skills your child is learning in school.

- Use this book as a homeschool curriculum. It will help with your homeschooling in the same way it helps parents that don't home-school—it supplements the third grade core curriculum.

- Challenge your child's teacher based on information you find here. ("Why isn't my child covering animal classification as it said in *Third Grade Success*?") Instead, look for the synergy in the information from both sources.

Use this book and its resources as supplemental information to enhance your child's third grade curriculum—and let's make it a good year for everyone!

Getting the Most for Your Third Grader

No parent says, "Oh, mediocre is okay for my child. Please do things halfway; it doesn't matter." Parents want the best for their children. This is not a matter of spending the most money on education or buying the latest educational toy. It is a matter of spending time with your child and expending effort to maximize what he or she is being provided by the school, by the community, and at home.

Getting the Most from Your School System

You wouldn't think twice about getting the most bang for your buck from a hotel, your gym, or a restaurant, and you shouldn't think twice about getting the most from your school system. The school system was designed to serve your needs, and you should take advantage of that.

Public Schools

Part of learning how to manage life as an adult is knowing how to manage interaction with bureaucratic agencies, so it makes sense that part of this learning take place within a kinder, gentler bureaucratic system. This is a good introduction to working within a system that was formed to assist in the development of children's abilities. Schools are also a workplace—with a chain of command—and that is a good induction into the workplace your child will enter as an adult. To further your children's educational experience, you and your children will have the opportunity to meet and work with:

- School personnel: your child's teacher, teacher's aides, specialists, the school counselor, the administrator or principal, and others

- Extracurricular groups: scouts, sports, after-school programs, and community parks and recreation programs

- Parents: of children from your child's class or grade level, school volunteers, and parent–teacher organizations

Participation in your child's education is paramount to his or her success. Active participation doesn't mean that you have to spend hours at the school as a volunteer, but it does include reading all of the communications your school sends either to you directly or home with your child. Also, read the school handbook and drop by your child's school on a regular basis if possible. If you can't stop by, check out the school or class Web site to see what units are being covered, any upcoming events, and so on. Participation means attending school events when you can, going to class parties when possible, and going to parent–teacher conferences. If they are scheduled at a time when you are not available, request a different time. The school administrator or principal usually requires that teachers try to accommodate your schedule.

The single most important thing you can do to get the most out of your local school system is to talk to your child's teacher. Find out what curricula your child will be covering and how you can help facilitate learning. Does the teacher see specific strengths and weaknesses that you can help enhance or bring up to speed? The teacher can help you identify your child's learning style, social skills, problem-solving abilities, and coping mechanisms.

Teachers play a role that extends outside the classroom. Your child's teacher is the perfect person to recommend systemwide and community resources. Teachers know how to find the local scout leaders, tutors, good summer programs, and community resources. Your child's teacher may be able to steer you in the right direction for getting your child on an intramural team. Teachers are truly partners in your child's upbringing.

Your child's teacher cares about your child's well-being. Everyone has heard stories about having a bad teacher or one who was "out to get my child." If that's the way you feel, then it's even more important to have regular conversations with the teacher. Maybe his or her actions or your child's actions are being misunderstood. In any case, your child's teacher is the main source of information about school and the gateway to resources for the year, so find a way to communicate.

If you know there is a problem with the teacher that needs to be taken seriously, try the following:

- Talk to parents with children in the class ahead of your child. They may be able to tell you how the issue was approached by parents the previous year—and they will have lots to tell about their experiences with teachers your child will have next year.

- Talk to your child's principal. This may result in your child being transferred to another class, so make sure you are prepared for that prior to making the appointment. Be willing to work with your child's current teacher prior to transferring your child. The less disruption your third grader experiences, the better.

- Talk to your local school administration center to see what the procedures are for transferring to another school. You will likely be required to provide transportation to a school outside of your home district, but if the problem is severe enough, it will be worth it.

No matter what, active participation and communication with your child's school is essential. It empowers you to:

- Accurately monitor your child's progress
- Determine which optional activities would enrich your child's learning experience
- Prepare your child for upcoming events, curricula, and skill introduction
- Share and add to the school learning environment
- Create a complementary learning environment in your home
- Spend time with your child

And just a word about the school secretary: this person knows more about what is going on in that building than anyone else. When I was a teacher, the school secretary always added to my and my students' success. The secretary is a taskmaster, nurse, mom or dad, and generally just a comforting figure in what can sometimes be a really big building. The school secretary always knows what forms to fill out, which teacher is where, what students are absent and why, when the next school event is, and how much candy money you owe for the latest fund-raiser. He or she is a source of lunch money, milk money, extra pencils, bus passes, and the copy machine. Get to know and love your school secretary.

Private Schools

On a micro level, participating in your child's education if she attends a private school isn't much different from participating if she attends a public school. Private schools have access to the same community resources. If you have a special needs child, the private school should work with local education agencies to see that your child gets the appropriate services. Through active communication and participation, you will derive the same benefits as parents whose children attend public school.

On a macro level, private schools are different from public schools. Private schools are governed not by a school board but by an internal system. This can be both easier and harder to navigate. Dealing with private schools is easier because the schools realize that you are paying tuition every month, so frankly they want to please their customers. Dealing with private schools is harder because they aren't accountable to the community for their actions nor are they governed by the same due processes as the public school system. Check out the school's administration hierarchy to see how decisions are made and what roles have been created for parent governance. Also, get to know the school's secretary.

To really be on top of things, it's a good idea to print a copy of your state's learning standards (see chapter 4) and familiarize yourself with the topics and skills that your state thinks third graders should learn. You can find a copy at www.knowledgeessentials.com. Compare the standards to those of your private school's third grade curriculum. If the curriculum is drastically different from the required state learning standards, your child will have difficulty passing the required state assessments. If your child's curriculum meets and exceeds the standards, your child will be well served by that school.

Private schools have the flexibility to incorporate religious elements or varied teaching philosophies that public schools can't provide. They are not subject to the separation of church and state requirements. Private schools operate without depending on community support (such as bond proposals); so as long as their tuition-paying constituency approves of their methods and the students who graduate from the programs demonstrate success, private schools can implement teaching methods at will that fall out of the mainstream.

Getting the Most from Your Homeschool Curriculum

A little power is a dangerous thing. You are homeschooling your child because you want more control over what and how your child learns and the environment in which he learns it. That is admirable, but don't be fooled. To a large extent, your child's natural ability to learn certain things at certain times will dictate the way you should approach any homeschool curriculum (chapters 2 and 3 explain this more fully). The best thing you can do when starting to homeschool your child is look at books on child development. Start with these:

- *Children's Strategies: Contemporary Views of Cognitive Development*, edited by David F. Bjorklund. Hillsdale, N.J.: Erlbaum Associates, 1990.

- *Piaget's Theory: Prospects and Possibilities*, edited by Harry Beilin. Hillsdale, N.J.: Erlbaum Associates, 1992.

- *Instructional Theories in Action: Lessons Illustrating Selected Theories and Models*, edited by Charles M. Reigeluth. Hillsdale, N.J.: Erlbaum Associates, 1987.

- *All Our Children Learning*, Benjamin S. Bloom. New York: McGraw-Hill, 1981.

You don't have to homeschool your child all by yourself or by limiting yourself to a particular homeschool organization's materials. Each state has some form of a regional education system with centers open to the public. At your public school system's curriculum resource center, you can check out curriculum materials and supplemental materials. Most of these centers have a workroom with things like a die press that cuts out letters and shapes from squares to animals to holiday items. Regional education centers often provide continuing education for teachers, so they usually have some training materials on hand. Look for information about your regional center on your state department of education's Web site. You can find a link to your state department of education at www.knowledgeessentials.com.

You can purchase homeschool curriculum kits designed to provide your child with a lion's share of the materials needed to complete a grade level. You can also buy subject area–specific curricula. It is important to ask the company that sells the curriculum to correlate the materials with your state's learning standards so that you can see which standards you need to reinforce with additional activities. You can find the companies that sell these kits at www.knowledgeessentials.com.

Using Supplemental Materials

You cannot expect any single curriculum in any public school, private school, or homeschool to meet all of the learning standards for the grade level and subject area in your state. Many will meet 90 percent of the standards and some will meet 75 percent, which is why there are supplemental materials. Schools use them and so should you. They are simply extra materials that help your child learn more. Examples of these materials include:

- Trade books. These are just books that are not textbooks or work-books—in other words, the kinds of books, fiction and nonfiction, that you would check out at the library or that your child would choose at a bookstore. Trade books don't have to tell about many things in a limited number of pages so they can tell a lot more about a single topic than a textbook can. They give your child a chance to practice skills that she is learning. If you choose wisely, you can find books that use newly learned reading skills, such as compound words, blends, prefixes and suffixes, or rhyming. Sometimes these skills will be set in the context of newly learned science or social studies topics, such as weather, habitats, or your community. Many companies provide these types of books for sale, but the most recognizable one may be Scholastic, Inc. Appendix A lists some books that are really good for third graders.

- Software and the Internet. Schools choose electronic activities and content, such as educational software and Internet sites, and electronic components, such as Leapfrog's LeapMat, allowing your child to expand his content knowledge while implementing skills just learned. Supplementing what your child is learning at school with these resources helps him gain technology skills within a familiar context. If you choose wisely, such as starting with the software choices listed in appendix B of this book, you can sometimes enhance reading skills and/or supplement a social studies or science topic while your child learns to operate a computer—talk about bang for your buck.

- Other materials. Videos, photographs, audio recordings, newspapers—just about anything you can find that helps expand what your child is learning is a supplemental resource. Loosely defined, supplemental resources can include a wide array of materials; your newly trained eye is limited only to what you now know is appropriate for your child.

Now you know what we need to cover, so let's get to it.

Third Grade Development

2

The journey begins. Good teachers base their activities on the developmental stages at which their students are performing. What is a developmental stage and why is it important?

The ability to learn is always related to your child's stage of intellectual development. Developmental stages describe how a child thinks and learns in different growth periods. These periods are loosely defined by age but are more accurately defined by behavior. They are important because children cannot learn something until physical growth gives them certain abilities; children who are at a certain stage cannot be taught the concepts of a higher stage (Brainerd, 1978).

The theory of child development that is the basis for modern teaching was formed by Jean Piaget, who was born in 1896 in Neuchâtel, Switzerland, and died in 1980. His theories have been expanded by other educators but stand as the foundation of today's classroom.

Piaget's Stages of Cognitive Development

Piaget is best known for his stages of cognitive development. He discovered that children think and reason differently at different periods in their lives, and he believed that everyone passes through a sequence of four distinct stages in exactly the same order, but the times in which children pass through them can vary by years. Piaget also described two processes that people use from infancy through adulthood to adapt: assimilation and accommodation. *Assimilation* is the process of using the environment to place information in a category of things you know. *Accommodation* is the process of using the environment to add a new category of things you know. Both tools are implemented throughout life and can be used together to understand a new piece of information.

Okay, did you assimilate and accommodate that? The main thing Piaget tells us is that kids really can't learn certain information and skills until they reach a certain place in their growth that is determined by years and behaviors. Understanding Piaget's stages is like getting the key to Learning City because it is a behavior map that tells you what your kids are ready to learn. Let's define the stages, then look at the behaviors. Piaget's four stages of cognitive development are:

1. *Sensorimotor stage (0 to 4 years):* In this period, intelligence is demonstrated through activity without the use of symbols (letters and numbers). Knowledge of the world is limited because it is based on actual experiences or physical interactions. Physical development (mobility) allows children to cultivate new intellectual abilities. Children will start to recognize some letters and numbers toward the end of this stage.

2. *Preoperational stage (4 to 7 years):* Intelligence is demonstrated through the use of oral language as well as letters and numbers. Memory is strengthened and imagination is developed. Children don't yet think logically very often, and it is hard for them to reverse their thinking on their own. Your little angel is still pretty egocentric at this age, and that is normal.

3. *Concrete operational stage (7 to 11 years):* As children enter this stage, they begin to think logically and will start to reverse

thinking on their own—for example, they will begin to complete inverse math operations (checking addition with subtraction, etc.). Expressing themselves by writing becomes easier. Logical thinking and expression is almost always about a concrete object, not an idea. Finally, children begin to think about other people more—they realize that things happen that affect others either more or less than they affect themselves.

4. *Formal operational stage (11 years and up):* As children become formally operational, they are able to do all of the things in the concrete operational stage—but this time with ideas. Children are ready to understand concepts and to study scientific theories instead of scientific discoveries. They can learn algebra and other math concepts not represented by concrete objects that can be counted. Whereas every stage until now has continuously moved forward, this is the only stage where a step back occurs. As a teenager, your child will become egocentric once again. It won't be easy for you. Thinking and acting as if the world exists exclusively for him or her is cute behavior for a five-year-old; it is rarely cute for a teenager.

Unfortunately, only 35 percent of high school graduates in industrialized countries obtain formal operations; many people will not ever think formally. However, most children can be taught formal operations.

The graph on page 16 puts the stages in a clear perspective.

Developmental Goals for Eight-Year-Olds

Now that you know the basic developmental indicators, let's get down to the nitty-gritty of what can be expected from your third grader. An eight-year-old can/will:

- Work quickly with a limited attention span
- Need physical release of energy

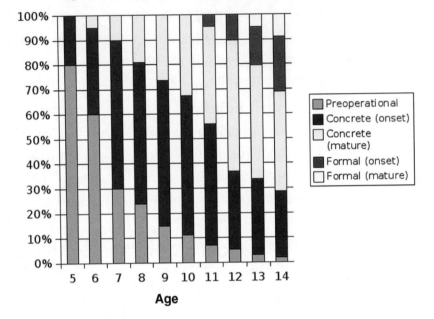

Percentage of Students in Piagetian Stages

- Be highly social
- Create friendships that are more inclusive than at age seven but will still prefer the same gender
- Cooperate and work well in groups
- Overestimate abilities and bite off more than he or she can chew
- Exhibit resiliency and bounce back quickly from mistakes
- Listen attentively but will be so full of ideas that he or she will not always be able to recall what has been said
- Enjoy explaining ideas in detail
- Exaggerate
- Begin to master basic academic skills and feel a sense of competence with cognitive skills

Your eight-year-old is trying very hard to master the skills to which he or she has been introduced. This means concentrating on handwriting, arts and crafts, computers, drawing, and other skills. If the accomplishments don't come easy, there is a tendency to exaggerate feelings of inferiority. Redirection is the best solution. Criticizing your eight-year-old will have an impact that you will regret for years. Schoolwork and supplemental activities are better if short and to the point. Accomplishments should be displayed: cover every inch of your refrigerator with your child's latest and greatest. Eight-year-olds benefit from graphing or charting accomplishments so that they can be reminded of successes while seeing the progression toward mastering a goal.

Developmental Goals for Nine-Year-Olds

Some third graders will turn nine during the school year. A nine-year-old can/will:

- Be industrious and impatient
- Be more coordinated than an eight-year-old
- Push himself to physical limits
- Fatigue easily and be prone to injury
- Be aloof
- Create exclusive friendship groups
- Prefer the same gender
- Be competitive
- Want to choose work partners
- Criticize herself and others
- Be discouraged easily
- See adult inconsistencies and imperfections
- Complain about fairness issues

- Love vocabulary and language play (but baby talk may reemerge)
- State things as negatives: "I hate it," "I can't," "boooring," "yeah, right"
- Be a concrete learner, but increasingly will be able to deal with multiple variables

Nine-year-olds tend to be more competitive. Although they are usually more coordinated than eight-year-olds, they often fatigue easily and complain about injuries, both real and imagined. They like to work with partners of their choice and might begin forming exclusive groups. They can be impatient, anxious, and easily discouraged. They generally don't like to take risks and they don't like to be wrong.

Now, you may be thinking, Oh no! My child is all over both lists! Remember, children vary greatly. It is common to find a two-and-a-half-year difference in development among children. Eight- to nine-year-olds who lag in specific skills often compensate by exceeding expectations in other areas of development. Don't worry. The best indicator of whether a child is in danger of falling behind is the rate of growth rather than an inventory of skills. If your child is making progress along the rough developmental continuum, don't be overly concerned about a few skills here and there.

Third Grade Learning 3

If you write it on the chalkboard, they will learn it. Sound familiar? If you are lucky, it doesn't—but for a great majority of people it is exactly how they were taught and were expected to learn. Luckily, in most schools, education has come to embrace children with different learning styles.

Learning Styles

Learning styles define how your child learns and processes information. Education experts have identified three main types of learning: visual, auditory, and physical. When learning a new math concept, for example, a visual learner will grasp the material more quickly by reading about it in a book or watching his or her teacher solve a problem on the blackboard. An auditory learner will understand the concept if she can listen to the teacher explain it and then answer questions. A physical learner (also known as tactile-kinesthetic) may need to use blocks, an abacus, or other counting materials (also known as manipulatives) to practice the new concept.

If you understand that your child is a visual learner most of the time—that is, he is most comfortable using sight to explore the world—you can play to his strength and incorporate physical and auditory learning styles when appropriate. It isn't unusual to interchange learning styles for different subjects. An auditory learner can easily use kinesthetic strategies to comprehend new math concepts.

Studies have shown that accommodating a child's learning style can significantly increase his performance at school. In 1992, the U.S. Department of Education found that teaching to a child's learning style was one of the few strategies that improved the scores of special education students on national tests. Identifying your child's learning styles and helping him within that context may be the single most significant factor in his academic achievement. Each activity in the subject area chapters of this book lists variations that help you tailor the activity to your child's learning style. Look for the symbols by the name of each learning style and use these styles to tailor the activities to your child's needs.

Learning styles are pretty easy to spot. All you have to do is watch your child's behavior when given a new piece of information.

👁 Visual

Would you give your right arm to get your child to listen to you? Are your walls a mural comprising every crayon your child has held? If you answered yes, you have a visual learner. You may not be able to get your child to follow two-step oral directions, but she can probably comprehend complex instructions when they are written on the blackboard or listed. Diagrams and graphs are a breeze. Your child can retell complex stories just by looking at one or two pictures from a book. Why is your child seemingly brilliant on paper but a space case when listening? Visual learners rely primarily on their sense of sight to take in information, understand it, and remember it. As long as they can see it, they can comprehend it.

Technically there are two kinds of visual learners: picture learners and print learners. Most children are a mixture of both, although some are one or the other (Willis and Hodson, 1999). Picture learners think in images; if you ask them what sound "oy" makes, they will likely think of a picture of a boy or a toy to remember the sounds of the letters. These kids like to draw—but you knew that by looking at your walls, right? Print learners think in language symbols: letters, numbers, and words. They would think of the actual letters "oy" to remember the sound they make together. Print learners learn to read quickly and are good spellers right off the bat. They also like to write.

Auditory

Is your child a talker? Is total silence the kiss of death to her concentration? Auditory learners understand new ideas and concepts best when they hear and talk about the information. If you observe a group of kids, auditory learners are the ones who learn a tune in a snap just from hearing someone sing it, or who can follow directions to the letter after being told only once or twice what to do. Some auditory learners concentrate better on a task when they have music or noise in the background, or retain new information more accurately when they talk it out. If you ask auditory learners what sound "oy" makes, they will recall the sound first and as many words as possible with that sound almost automatically.

Kinesthetic

Does your child need to touch everything? Physical learners (also known as tactual-kinesthetic learners—*tactual* for touch, *kinesthetic* for movement) use their hands or bodies to absorb new information. In some ways, everyone is a physical learner. If you peek into a classroom, you will see the physical learner tapping a pencil, a finger, or a foot, or twirling her hair to help her concentrate. These kids can't sit still and they are in the top percentile for being diagnosed with attention deficit disorder (ADD).

Before you run to the doctor because your child can't sit still, carefully observe him over a long period of time. Is the movement productive? Does he absorb or block information when moving? If he prefers to feel things in his hands or performs steady movement when trying to concentrate, he is engaging in productive learning.

Physical learners enjoy hands-on activities, such as cutting construction paper, sorting objects with their hands, and building elaborate projects. When you ask physical learners what sound "oy" makes, they will think of the physical cues used by the teacher or the cues they used when learning, such as tapping, physically picking the letters out of the alphabet, or holding *o* and *y* blocks.

Cognitive Learning

Cognitive learning levels are another way that teachers describe how a child processes information. I hear you asking, "Wow, how much of this do I have to remember?"—and you know I am going to say all of it, but it is really important. Let's recap for a minute to see how all of this fits together.

First, you learned about developmental stages, the physical growth that needs to happen before your child can learn certain things. Second, you learned about learning styles, the way your child prefers to process information. Third, you are about to learn about cognitive learning levels, the levels at which your child knows, understands, and can use information that he or she learns. Piaget identified the developmental stages in the 1930s and 1940s. By the 1950s, a group of researchers got together, led by Benjamin Bloom, and created the cognitive learning taxonomy designed to help you understand the levels of learning that can occur with new information. Bloom is often considered one of the most important educational theorists of the twentieth century. He was a professor at the University of Chicago who was more than a brilliant teacher: he was a brilliant thinker. Bloom spent his career researching how thinking and learning happened in students of all ages. Bloom and his researchers broke down the learning levels as follows:

Level 1: Knowledge. The things you know—bits of information that you can memorize, such as the ABCs.

Level 2: Comprehension. The things you understand—knowing the ABCs and understanding that they represent sounds.

Level 3: Application. The things you can apply—knowing the ABCs, understanding that they represent sounds, and then sounding out a word.

Level 4: Analysis. The things you understand well enough to think about them in a new way—knowing the ABCs, understanding that they represent sounds, sounding out a word, and then figuring out what the word means.

Level 5: Synthesis. Understanding something well enough to apply it to a new situation—knowing the ABCs, understanding that they represent sounds, sounding out a word, figuring out what the word means, and using it in a new way.

Level 6: Evaluation. Understanding something so well that you can tell if it is being used correctly—knowing the ABCs, understanding that they represent sounds, sounding out a word, figuring out what the word means, using it in a new way, and then figuring out if the new way is right.

Check the Bloom's Cognitive Learning Levels table on page 24 for some specific key words and behaviors for each level. Getting to know the key words will help you determine how to ask your child questions in order to find out the level at which your child understands new information. Use the examples in the right-hand column of the table to ask questions that check for each level of understanding.

Bloom's Cognitive Learning Levels

Cognitive Level	Verb	Key Words		Examples
Knowledge Recalls data. Exhibits memory of previously learned material by recalling facts and basic concepts.	Remember	choose define describe find how identify knows label list match name omit outline recall	recognize reproduce select show spell state tell what when where which who why	• Defines terminology/vocabulary • Describes details and elements • Recognizes classifications and categories • Knows principles, generalizations, theories, models, and structures • Knows subject-specific skills, algorithms, techniques, and methods • Names criteria for using certain procedures • Spells words • Outlines facts, events, stories, or ideas
Comprehension Demonstrates understanding of facts and ideas by organizing, comparing, translating, interpreting, giving descriptions, and stating main ideas. Understands the meaning, translation, interpolation, and interpretation of instructions and problems.	Understand	classify compare comprehend contrast convert defend demonstrate distinguish estimate explain extend illustrate	infer interpret outline paraphrase predict relate rephrase rewrite show summarize translate	• Summarizes or retells information • Translates an equation • Outlines the main ideas • Summarizes instructions, facts, details, or other things • Compares and contrasts ideas • Explains what is happening • Identifies statements to support a conclusion • Classifies information

Bloom's Cognitive Learning Levels

Cognitive Level	Verb	Key Words		Examples
Application Solves problems in new situations by applying acquired knowledge, facts, techniques, and rules in a different way. Uses a concept in a new situation or unprompted use of an abstraction. Applies what was learned in the classroom into novel situations.	Apply	apply build change choose compute construct demonstrate develop discover identify interview manipulate	model modify operate plan predict prepare produce relate select show solve utilize	• Applies a formula to solve a problem • Uses a manual to solve a problem • Describes how to use something • Finds examples to help apply ideas, rules, steps, or an order • Describes a result • Modifies ideas, rules, steps, or an order for use in another way • Selects facts to demonstrate something
Analysis Examines and breaks information into parts by identifying motives or causes. Makes inferences and finds evidence to support generalizations. Separates material or concepts into component parts so that its organizational structure may be understood. Distinguishes between facts and inferences.	Analyze	analyze assume categorize classify compare conclusion contrast discover dissect distinction distinguish	divide examine function inference inspect list motive relationships take part in test for theme	• Troubleshoots a problem using logical deduction • Lists components or parts of a whole • Names the function of something • Makes a distinction between two or more things • Classifies or categorizes a number of things • Draws a conclusion • Lists the parts of a whole

(continued)

Bloom's Cognitive Learning Levels *(continued)*

Cognitive Level	Verb	Key Words		Examples
Synthesis Compiles information in a different way by combining elements in a new pattern or proposing alternative solutions. Builds a structure or pattern from diverse elements. Puts parts together to form a whole, with emphasis on creating a new meaning or structure.	Create	adapt arrange build categorize change choose combine compile compose construct create delete design develop devise discuss elaborate estimate explain formulate generate happen imagine improve	invent make up maximize minimize modify organize original originate plan predict propose rearrange reconstruct relate reorganize revise rewrite solution solve summarize suppose tell test write	• Integrates training from several sources to solve a problem • Formulates a theory • Invents a solution • Constructs a model • Compiles facts • Minimizes or maximizes an event or item • Designs a solution, model, or project • Adapts something to create another thing
Evaluation Presents and defends opinions by making judgments about information, validity of ideas, or quality of work based on a set of criteria.	Evaluate	agree appraise assess award choose compare conclude criteria	importance influence interpret judge justify mark measure opinion	• Selects the most effective solution • Explains a selection, conclusion, or recommendation • Prioritizes facts • Rates or ranks facts, characters (people), or events • Assesses the value or importance of something

Bloom's Cognitive Learning Levels

Cognitive Level	Verb	Key Words		Examples
Evaluation (continued) Makes judgments about the value of ideas or materials.		criticize decide deduct defend determine disprove dispute estimate evaluate explain	perceive prioritize prove rank rate recommend rule on select support value	• Justifies a selection, conclusion, or recommendation

Adapted from Benjamin S. Bloom, *Taxonomy of Educational Objectives: The Classification of Educational Goals, by a Committee of College and University Examiners* (New York: Longmans, Green, 1956).

The Standards   4

Standards-based education came into the national spotlight over a decade ago. Communities and school districts previously made their own curriculum choices. For example, in one school district civics was taught in eighth grade and in another district it was taught in ninth grade, resulting in uneven and low test scores, because children were not taught the same subjects in the same grades but were tested on the same subjects.

The idea behind the standards reform movement is straightforward: when states set clear standards defining what a child should know and be able to do in certain grades, teachers and learners are able to focus their efforts and highlight particular areas in which they need improvement. Ideally, the standards show teachers what they need to teach by allowing curricula and assessments that measure performance to be aligned with the standards.

As with all reform movements, there are people who disagree with the idea of creating common learning standards. They primarily point to tendencies to simply "teach the test" and complain that the standards limit content breadth and community input. The real gripe may lie in the fact that education has always been a local issue. It is easy to fear change when you fear community values may be lost by standard-izing state curriculum. Others believe that standards even the playing field. Before you form your own opinion, let's take a look at standards-based education.

Standards-based education lists content and skills that children need to learn at each grade level. Success depends on combining content and performance standards with consistent curriculum and instruction as well as appropriate assessment and accountability. This is the point where teachers and learners start to feel anxious. Everything sounds very official, particularly the accountability part. What does this language mean and what happens if children don't meet learning standards requirements?

Relax—there are no learning standards police patrolling our neighborhood schools, libraries, and bookstores. There are simply baselines by which the state determines eligibility for a high school diploma.

Let's start by defining learning standards.

Types of Learning Standards

Learning standards are broad statements that describe what content a child should know and what skills a child should be able to do in different subject areas.

Content standards are a form of learning standards that describe the topics to be studied, not the skills to be performed.

Performance standards are a form of learning standards that describe the skills to be performed, not the content to be studied.

Public school teachers must ensure that their students are taught the required content and skills because they are accountable not only to the students but also to their state, their school district, and their community for every child's performance on test scores. Private schools are accountable to their constituency with respect to student performance but not to the public. In fact, school requirements as well as teacher licensure are not as strictly monitored for private schools. The academically strong private schools institute internal standards that meet or exceed state expectations for public schools, but there are private schools that feel other aspects of child development, such as religious development, take precedence over academics. If your child attends private school, you must research the school to make sure it meets your expectations both academically and socially.

The use of testing to monitor classroom instruction is central to the theory of standards-based reform. It assumes that educators and the public can agree on what should be taught, that a set of clear standards can be developed, which in turn drive curriculum and instruction, and that tests can measure how well students perform based on those standards. There are two main types of standardized testing that your child will encounter:

1. Tests to determine individual student eligibility for promotion and graduation, college admission, or special honors. This type of testing has a long history. Examples include high school exit exams and college entrance exams, such as the Scholastic Aptitude Test (SAT) and the Advanced Placement (AP) test.

2. Tests that measure and compare school, school district, statewide, and national performance for broad public accountability. Increasingly, policy makers at the federal, state, and local levels want to identify ways to measure student performance in order to see how well the public education system is doing its job. The goals of this accountability approach include providing information about the status of the educational system, motivating desired change, measuring program effectiveness, and creating systems for financially sanctioning schools and requiring educators to receive more training based on the performance of their students.

It makes sense for you to make sure the content and skills that you work on with your child match the content and skills that the state has identified for that grade level. Children will do better on the standardized tests when more learning standards match assessment, or test, requirements. Legislation is in place that requires states to align their learning expectations with their testing expectations. The disconnect came when federal requirements for learning standards preceded testing requirements. Many states took the opportunity to test for content and skills that seemed more important than the ones enumerated in the learning standards. States and schools are working under federal guidelines to make all of the content match in a few years.

Learning Standards Resources

Each state has created a document that describes what children are supposed to know and what they are supposed to be able to do at each grade level and in each subject area. You may wonder who writes the standards and why you should believe that these people know what is best. A lot of public school teachers have wondered the same thing.

You can rest assured that writing the state learning standards is a collaborative effort. Most states rely on input from experts who know about the grade level and subject area. These experts could include teachers, researchers, people from the education industry, and school administrators. As an endnote or a footnote, each document lists the people hired by the state to help write the final version.

You can locate the standards that apply to your child through your state Department of Education's Internet site, by calling your state Department of Education, or through the Internet at www .knowledgeessentials.com. There are several things you should read for:

1. *Content standards*: What topics will your child be studying?

2. *Performance standards*: What skills must your child develop by the end of the year?

3. *Resources*: What resources are designed to help teachers meet the learning standards? Can you access them?

4. *Correlation reports*: Does the state provide a listing of how the required textbooks and other materials meet their own learning standards? Your school district should also be able to provide you with this information.

As you read your state's learning standards document, you may notice that you don't always agree with what is listed for your child to be learning. Is there anything you can do?

If your child attends a public school, there is little you can do to protest the prescribed curricula, but you can certainly enhance the curricula through learning activities at home. If your child attends a private school, you may have greater influence over classroom activities (as a paying customer), but you will probably not get the curricula changed to meet your concerns.

If you teach your child at home, then you have as much control as you would like over your child's curricula. You undoubtedly have specific beliefs that have led you to decide to homeschool, and you can remain true to those beliefs while still covering the required curricula. Even if you don't believe the required curricula are entirely appropriate, the assessments required by the states and higher education institutions will be normed to the learning standards of the state in which you live. The standards are just the basics that your child will need to succeed in mainstream society. There are many more opportunities for learning across a wide range of subjects that can be totally up to you.

Third Grade Reading

5

As a third grader your child is not only learning to read but is also reading to learn (reading for content as well as enjoyment). Reading will become a part of every subject or class your child participates in from now to adulthood. Teachers expect third graders to read lessons and chapters on their own and to be ready to discuss them in class. Children feel a sense of accomplishment when they remember what they have read and are prepared for class.

Your child will be working on reading skills during the beginning part of the school day. Because reading affects learning in all the other subjects, it is important to focus on it at the beginning of the day when your child is rested and ready to learn.

Third grade reading will build on the mechanics of reading and comprehension skills your child learned in second grade (see the table on page 36). Fluency also continues to be important as your child needs to be able to read most words without having to sound them out in order to understand or comprehend the text.

Beginning of Third Grade Reading Checklist

Students who are working at the standard level at the beginning of third grade:

_____ Read with understanding and fluency

_____ Figure out unknown words in context

_____ Recognize word patterns (prefixes and suffixes)

_____ Communicate in written form

_____ Retell stories with accuracy

_____ Correct themselves while reading

_____ Identify and spell many words

_____ Recognize parts of a story

_____ Read for more than pleasure

_____ Utilize a larger sight vocabulary

Third graders will also work on building their vocabulary—the words they can read and define.

Mechanics of Reading Skills	Comprehension Skills
Recognizes word patterns such as contractions and compound words	Reads with fluency and understanding
Utilizes a larger sight vocabulary	Uses punctuation cues to help with phrasing and to determine meaning
Uses knowledge of synonyms, antonyms, and homonyms to determine word meaning	Makes predictions about the text
Figures out unknown words in context	Analyzes the characters; this may include their traits, feelings, relationships, and changes they go through
	Summarizes the text by recognizing the main idea and details

The Mechanics of Reading

Reading mechanics are the nuts and bolts of reading words and sentences. Mechanical skills determine the size of the words that your child can read, the frequency with which he or she can read the harder words, and the rate at which he or she reads.

Selecting Reading Material

To help your child with reading, you need to use appropriate books. There are various reading levels within each grade level. Books are coded to tell you the reading level and what it means. You will find reading suggestions in appendix A of this book. You can also go to www.knowledgeessentials.com to see a list of these books and learn how to use them to teach your child. It is a good idea to encourage your child to choose different genres of books. Some genres to choose from include realistic fiction, historical fiction, nonfiction, science fiction, fantasy, poetry, fairy tales, and fables.

Newspapers and magazines are good tools for practicing reading. Not only are children practicing their reading skills, but they are also learning about the world we live in. The articles they read can lead to some great family discussions or debates, which are important to the learning process. Discussions will help your child express and defend his or her opinions on many subjects, which also comes in handy in the classroom.

Vocabulary

Children not only have to be able to read words, they also have to know what the words mean. If your child has a large vocabulary, she will be able to comprehend more of the text as she reads. The English language can be very confusing. There are homonyms (words that sound the same but have different meanings and spellings, such as dear and deer), synonyms (different words that have the same meaning, such as huge and large), and antonyms (different words that have opposite meanings, such as far and near). Thankfully there are many resources to help make sense of the English language. Some of these resources include a dictionary and a thesaurus as well as many other specialty books.

Third grade reading focuses on using these vocabulary builders:

- Contractions

- Compound words

- Synonyms, homonyms, and antonyms

Contractions

Contractions are a short way to write and say words. You form contractions by leaving out one or more letters and replacing them with an apostrophe. As an adult you read, write, and say contractions automatically, but reading and writing them are new to your third grader. Using contractions in everyday speech is pretty easy, and your child has likely mastered that. Now, and most important, your child needs to learn what contractions look like and that the apostrophe takes the place of the missing letters.

Discuss what a contraction is with your child. Remember that *contraction* is a word that has several meanings. A friend and third grade teacher reminisced about a student who told her and the class that a contraction was "those pains my mom had when she had my baby brother."

Determining the meaning of a verbal contraction lies in knowing the complete words for the shortened form. The following are examples of some common contractions:

don't = do not

I'm = I am

he's = he is

let's = let us

we've = we have

they're = they are

aren't = are not

weren't = were not

Remind your child not to confuse contractions with possessive pronouns. For example, *it's* means "it is," not "belonging to it."

Incorrect: The team gathered *it's* equipment and boarded the bus.

Correct: The team gathered *its* equipment and boarded the bus.

An apostrophe may be used to omit letters or numbers at the beginning of words or dates:

'90s = 1990s

'cause = because (slang; not proper in most writing)

Note that *o'clock* stands for "of the clock," an expression that's become completely replaced by its contraction.

Compound Words

A compound word is made by combining two or more words to form a new word. Unlike in a contraction, however, none of the letters are replaced by apostrophes.

There are three forms of compound words:

1. The closed form, in which the words are melded together, such as firefly, secondhand, softball, childlike, redhead, keyboard, makeup, notebook

2. The hyphenated form, such as daughter-in-law, over-the-counter, six-year-old, mass-produced

3. The open form, such as post office, real estate, middle class, full moon, half sister

In the life of a third grader, the only form of compound word is the closed form. Compound words are pretty easy to figure out if you know what the words mean individually. Usually you can use the meaning of the two words to identify the meaning of the new word. For example, lunch + box = lunchbox. Your child is likely to know right away that a lunchbox is a box that holds a lunch. The table on page 40 describes some important skills related to the mechanics of reading, where children can run into problems, and what you can do to help them along.

Synonyms, Homonyms, and Antonyms

It is hard enough to remember these word relationships on our own; now we have to remember them in front of our kids! As a reminder:

- Synonyms are words with the same meaning. *Two, pair,* and *couple* are synonyms.

- Homonyns are words that sound the same but are spelled differently and mean different things. *To, too,* and *two* are homonyms.

- Antonyms are words with the opposite meaning. *Hot* and *cold* are antonyms.

The easiest way to identify a synonym, a homonym, and an antonym is by thinking of the meaning of the words that you are working with and what you are trying to convey. If you are looking for a word that means the same as another word, or if you see two words

Mechanics of Reading Skills	Having Problems?	Quick Tips
Writes contractions properly.	Forgets to put the apostrophe in the proper place.	Usually the letter that is left out is a vowel. Practice writing the word and the contraction beside each other. The apostrophe goes where the letter(s) is left out.
Comfortably uses compound words.	Has difficulty understanding or remembering the meaning of compound words.	Draw pictures that represent each part of the compound word: a picture for the first part, the second part, and the whole word.
Uses contractions at the appropriate time.	Uses contractions in place of possessive nouns (or vice versa).	Read the word *it's* as the two words *it is*. If it makes sense as two words, use the contraction; if not, it is a possessive.
Identifies and uses homonyms correctly.	Uses the homonym spelling that doesn't fit; uses the wrong homonym.	Make flash cards with a picture and a sentence that show each way to use the words. Play Concentration with the flash cards.
Distinguishes between synonyms and antonyms.	Has trouble remembering the difference between synonyms and antonyms.	Connect the word *similar* to the word *synonym* by teaching your child to ask himself, "Am I trying to think of a word that is similar to the word I am seeing?" or "Is this word similar to the other word?" If the answer is yes, he is looking for a synonym. If the answer is no, he is looking for an antonym.

that mean the same thing, then you know whether the words are synonyms or antonyms. The point is to focus on how the words relate before focusing on what they mean if you are working with them in a grammatical context.

Mechanics of Reading Activities

1 Contraction Hunt

TIME: 20–30 minutes

MATERIALS
- newspaper
- highlighters
- rounded-edge scissors
- nontoxic glue
- paper
- pencils

Learning happens when: your child takes the newspaper and highlights as many contractions as he can find. When your child has finished highlighting, have him cut the contractions out. Beside each contraction have your child write the word or words that the contraction is made from. You can draw columns on a piece of paper if you like and let your child glue the contractions in the first column and write the words in the second column.

Variations: To add a step for practice, take the paper and cut it into individual pieces so that it becomes a reusable matching game. Paste the individual pieces onto tag board to make them sturdier.

 This is naturally appealing to your kinesthetic learner. After your child has done the activity as a matching game several times, add a time limit to it.

👁 This is also a good activity for a visual learner because your child is able to see the word as two parts as well as the contraction.

👂 If your child learns best by hearing, ask your child to say each word as he is working on the activity.

Mastery occurs when: your child correctly identifies the two words that make up each contraction.

You may want to help your child a little more if: he is having trouble identifying the two words that the contraction stands for. Start with fewer contractions, and once he has mastered those, slowly add more until he can work with all of the contractions.

2 Contraction Sentences

TIME: 20–30 minutes

MATERIALS

▪ pencils
▪ list of contractions (if you need a list of contractions, you can find one at www .knowledgeessentials.com)
▪ index cards

Learning happens when: your child writes a sentence using one contraction on one of the index cards. On the other side of the index card, she then writes the same sentence, only this time replacing the contraction with the word or words it represents. You can keep the cards to use as flash cards at a later time.

Variations: If you don't want to use index cards, use a dry erase board. Most kids like to use erase boards. The only drawback is you won't have flash cards for future use.

✋ Your kinesthetic learner will like this activity best with the dry erase board because she will be active while writing and then erasing.

👁 This activity is also good for your visual learner because she can see everything at once on the erase board rather than having to flip the index cards.

👂 If your child learns best by hearing, ask her to read her sentence aloud and then repeat the contraction and the words it replaces.

Mastery occurs when: your child can correctly identify, use, and spell all of the contractions.

You may want to help your child a little more if: she is having trouble identifying the words that make up each contraction.

Start with fewer contractions and then add a new one after your child has mastered the previous contractions. Continue to add contractions until you have used all of them.

3 | Combining Words

Learning happens when: you have your child label the folder "Compound Words." Write one word from each of the compound words on an index card—for example, "cow" on one card and "boy" on another card (put them together and you have cowboy). Continue until you have enough cards for your child to combine and form compound words. Have him use the index cards to form compound words. As your child makes a compound word, have him write it on one of the sheets of paper. Then have him look the word up in the dictionary and write down its meaning on the sheet of paper. Discuss the meaning with your child. Have him write a sentence that uses the compound word. Put each completed sheet in the Compound Word folder. Continue until your child has made ten to fifteen entries in the Compound Word folder.

Variations: Ask your child to illustrate and color each page of words.

Ask your kinesthetic or visual learner to use the computer to write and illustrate the Compound Word book. Your child could use the clip art found in many word processing programs as is or draw the pictures himself. You can also find clip art at www.knowledgeessentials.com.

Ask your child to read his book aloud to you and others.

Mastery occurs when: your child is able to correctly identify the meaning of each compound word and use the word in a sentence.

TIME: 30–40 minutes

MATERIALS
- markers
- folder with brads
- list of compound words (if you need a list of compound words, you can find one at www .knowledgeessentials.com)
- index cards
- lots of paper that has been 3-hole-punched
- dictionary

You may want to help your child a little more if: he is having trouble combining words into compound words or if he either doesn't understand the meaning of the word or can't use it correctly in a sentence. You might want to make the first compound word and complete the first page of the folder as a model for your child to follow. Then have your child add two or three pages to the folder a day. Make sure each day you review the previous day's pages.

4 | The ABCs of Compound Words

TIME: 2 hours

MATERIALS
- pencils
- paper that has been 3-hole-punched
- crayons or colored pencils
- folder with brads

Learning happens when: you and your child brainstorm a list of compound words. When you have ten or fifteen compound words written down, your child will need to write the ABCs vertically on a piece of paper. Then decide what compound word should go with the appropriate letter of the alphabet. For example, A might stand for airplane and B might stand for baseball. (It is okay to skip some alphabet letters until your child has more practice.) When your child has decided what compound word will go with each letter, have her write each compound word and its definition on one of the sheets of paper. Your child can then illustrate each page to help her remember the meaning of each word. Place the papers in alphabetical order into the folder. Help your child design a cover with a title. She now has a book of compound words for review whenever she needs it.

Variations: Ask your child to use a word processing program on the computer to produce the book. She could use clip art for the illustrations. You can find some clip art at www.knowledge essentials.com.

✍ Your kinesthetic learner will like doing the variation on the computer. Your child will appreciate having her hands moving around and using the clip art program.

👁 This is a good activity for your visual learner because she is producing her own visual aid: a book.

👂 Ask your child to read her book aloud to an audience.

Mastery occurs when: your child successfully identifies the compound words' meanings.

You may want to help your child a little more if: she doesn't identify meanings of both parts of the word and relate them together. Try asking your child to draw a picture of each part of the word and then a picture of what the words mean when they are put together.

5 | Homonym Charades

Write a word from the list of homonyms and its definition on the same side of an index card, then write the homonym and its definition on another card. For example, both "bare" and "bear" would need to be included in the game. On the blank side you could label all of the cards "Homonym Charades," for future use.

Learning happens when: you place the cards with the blank side up in the center of the players. One player draws a card and acts out the meaning of the word on the card while the others try to guess the word. Remember, the player acting out the word can't talk. Whoever guesses the word writes the correct spelling on the dry erase board, then takes a turn drawing a card and acting it out. If no one guesses correctly, ask the "actor" to give you a hint or two. If no one still guesses correctly, put that card aside and have the player draw another. At the end of the game, talk about the card you set aside. Why was it so hard to guess? Are there different ways to act it out that may be easier to guess?

TIME: 30–40 minutes

MATERIALS
- pencils
- list of homonyms with definitions (if you need a list of homonyms, you can find one at www .knowledgeessentials.com)
- index cards
- markers
- dry erase board
- dry erase markers
- at least 2 players

Variations: Try keeping track of points: one point for guessing the word correctly and another point for spelling it correctly. You can also ask your child to write a sentence with the word or just say the sentence aloud.

✍ Your kinesthetic learner will love this activity because he can move around and write the word on the dry erase board.

👁 Ask your child to help prepare the cards and write the word and/or sentence on the dry erase board. He might even want to draw on the card a picture that illustrates the meaning of the word.

👂 Ask your child to say the word and/or sentence aloud. It would be a good idea to also have him spell the word aloud.

Mastery occurs when: your child successfully associates the correct spelling to the definition of each word.

You may want to help your child a little more if: he is having trouble identifying the correct word and its spelling. Start with fewer cards. When your child demonstrates mastery of those cards, add some more until he has mastered all of the cards.

6 | Homonym Sentences

TIME: 20–30 minutes

MATERIALS
▪ dictionary
▪ list of homonyms (if you need a list of homonyms, you can find one at www.knowledgeessentials.com)
▪ paper
▪ pencils

Learning happens when: you choose one pair of homonyms at a time to work with—for example, "ant" and "aunt." Your child should write a sentence using each word to demonstrate that she understands the meaning of the words. For example, "I watched an ant carry a piece of food to its anthill." "My aunt is a famous singer." If your child doesn't know a word well enough to write a sentence, ask her to look it up in the dictionary. Continue with the same process until you feel your child understands the concept. There are so many homonyms in the English language that it would be impossible to go over them all at once. So take your time and do this activity again when you feel your child is ready.

Variations: Choose homonyms that would be easy to organize into a funny story. Instead of just writing random sentences, have your child use the homonyms in a story.

 Your kinesthetic learner would enjoy beating a rhythm while rapping or singing her sentences to you.

👁 Your child might want to draw a small picture of the homonym to go with each sentence.

👂 Your auditory learner also might want to create a tune or a rap song of her sentences to sing to you or an audience.

Mastery occurs when: your child uses the correct homonyms in the sentences and spells them correctly.

You may want to help your child a little more if: she is not able to use each homonym correctly in a sentence. You might give your child a hint in the beginning until she is able to do it on her own.

7 | Synonym Race

Write the words from the list of synonyms on individual index cards and the dictionary definitions of the words on another set of cards. Make sure you have at least four or five words that have the same meaning. You might want to do this activity outside where you have plenty of room. Make sure it is not a windy day or you will spend more time chasing the cards than identifying the synonyms.

Learning happens when: you place the cards with the words only at one end of the yard. Make sure the cards are spread out with the words facing up so that you can see them. Stand at the other end

> **TIME: 20–30 minutes**
>
> **MATERIALS**
> ▪ markers
> ▪ list of synonyms with definitions (if you need a list of synonyms, you can find one at www .knowledgeessentials .com)
> ▪ index cards
> ▪ dictionary
> ▪ at least 2 players

of the yard with the definition cards and the participants. Read a definition to them. The players will then run to the other end and gather up as many words as they can find that correspond to the definition, run back, and check their words with you.

Variations: If you would rather do this activity indoors, try putting the words at the end of a hallway or using Velcro to attach them to a piece of poster board. (You can buy poster board and small circular self-sticking pieces of Velcro at any craft store.)

- This activity is very appealing to your kinesthetic learner because he is able to run back and forth.

- Your visual learner will like this activity because the words and the definitions are written, so he can see them.

- When auditory learners are choosing their words, they might also say the words aloud to reinforce their learning.

Mastery occurs when: your child can choose four or five words that match each definition that you read to him.

You may want to help your child a little more if: he is having trouble finding at least three synonyms for each definition. Start with fewer choices until your child can correctly identify those, then slowly add more synonym combinations.

8 | Synonym Switch

TIME: 20–30 minutes

MATERIALS
- short, simple newspaper article
- highlighters
- pencils
- paper

Go through the newspaper article and highlight words that your child can exchange with a synonym.

Learning happens when: you ask your child to replace each word with one of her own. Have her rewrite the article and read it aloud with the new words. If your child is successful, the article should still have the same meaning as it did before.

Variations: Ask your child to go through the article and highlight words to find synonyms for herself.

✋ Your child will like the variation where she does the highlighting.

👁 Your visual learner can use correcting fluid instead of a highlighter and write the synonym in the appropriate place with colored markers.

👂 Ask your child to say each word aloud before reading the entire article with the new words.

Mastery occurs when: your child can replace the words with the synonyms so that the article still makes sense when she reads it.

You may want to help your child a little more if: she has trouble finding the right synonyms. Try giving her a clue, such as the first letter of a word that would be a synonym.

9 Antonym Twister

Using markers, divide the sheet into a table with three columns and four rows. Write a word from the list of antonyms in one rectangle and its opposite in any other rectangle. The following table is an example of how your sheet might look.

TIME: 20–30 minutes

MATERIALS

▪ markers

▪ old white sheet

▪ list of antonyms (if you need a list of antonyms, you can find one at www .knowledgeessentials.com)

powerful (weak)	lose (find)	bitter (sweet)
whisper (shout)	open (close)	fearless (fearful/scared)
enter (exit)	ordinary (special or unique)	artificial (natural)
perfect (flawed)	wealthy (poor)	stormy (nice or calm)

Learning happens when: you play a Twister-type game with the antonyms. You play this game as you would Twister, except instead of calling out a color and a body part, you call out an antonym and a body part. Players match the word you call out to its antonym on the board and touch that match with the body part you called out. So, if your board contains the words in the sample table on page 49, the corresponding words that would be in your list of words to call out are the ones in parentheses.

Variations: Try playing the game without the twisting by having your child move his whole body to each rectangle. If you want to use the game board again, you might want to write the words on index cards and tape or Velcro them to the game board. This would allow you to practice with other words.

- Constant body movement makes this activity perfect for your kinesthetic child.
- Encourage your child to help you create the game board.
- Ask your child to repeat the word you call out, then say the word in the rectangle to which he moves.

Mastery occurs when: your child can correctly identify all of the antonym pairs. When this happens, you will want to change the game board.

You may want to help your child a little more if: he has a hard time identifying a word's antonym. You might want to start with a smaller game board with fewer rectangles and make sure you have discussed the meanings of each word with your child right before you begin the activity.

10 Antonym Match

Draw a table with five columns and five rows on a sheet of paper.

Learning happens when: your child writes one word from the list of antonyms in each rectangle of the grid. Then she should color two rectangles with words in them that are antonyms the same color. She should change colored pencils and color another two rectangles that are antonyms. Repeat the procedure until all of the squares are colored. The following table is an example of how your game board might look.

TIME: 20–30 minutes

MATERIALS

- paper
- colored pencils
- list of antonyms (if you need a list of antonyms, you can find one at www .knowledgeessentials.com)

big	bold	honest	bad	clean
rapid	filthy	boring	light	cruel
dark	different	**Antonym Match**	friendly	little
good	deceitful	gradual	smooth	coarse
exciting	moist	alike	arid	timid

Variations: When your child has completed the game board, she can write sentences containing some of the antonyms. Instead of coloring the rectangles, you could have her cover the rectangles with a bean or a paper clip and play a game like Bingo. The center space would be a free space.

✋ Your kinesthetic learner will enjoy coloring the rectangles or playing the game as a form of Bingo because in both versions she will be able to move around.

👁 The activity is good for your visual learner because the coloring helps her visualize the connection between the words.

👂 Ask your child to read the antonym pairs aloud.

Mastery occurs when: your child has correctly identified all of the pairs of antonyms. Since there are so many antonyms in the English language, you should repeat this activity with a new set of words.

You may want to help your child a little more if: she isn't able to identify all of the antonym pairs. Start with a smaller game board and fewer pairs until your child can identify them. Then you can introduce her to more pairs of antonyms.

Comprehension

Third graders can read and know the meaning of a lot of words. Now they should continue practicing by using all of the words they have learned in the context of a paragraph, an article, or a story. They need to be able to focus on the meaning as they read. Since they will be reading longer chapter books in the third grade, it is very important that they be able to remember what they have read from one day to the next.

Third graders can benefit from keeping a reading diary in which they can write about things in books they liked or disliked, things that made them sad, or things that reminded them of something in their own lives. This can help children remember stories a lot better. It also

Setting	The time and place of a story
Characters	The people in a story
Conflict	The main problem a character is facing
Resolution	How the character solves his or her problem
Sequence of events	The order of events that lead to the resolution of the problem

helps to discuss stories, asking questions about the story and the characters. Third graders are expected to be able to identify the parts of a story, as described in the table on page 52.

Remember how nice it was to cuddle up with your child and read him a bedtime story? If your child will still let you, do it until he won't. It is important for your child to listen to how you use expression and punctuation cues to help give meaning to the text. It's also just a good

Comprehension Skills	Having Problems?	Quick Tips
Makes predictions.	Continually says, "I don't know," or won't try.	Some children are afraid to be wrong. Let your child know it's okay to be wrong. You just want to get her to use her past experiences to help with understanding the text. Predicting is more like an opinion than an answer—you are right if you try.
Identifies parts of the story.	Can't remember what each part is called.	Make a poster or flash cards with a question for each part. • Setting: Where and when? • Characters: Who? • Conflict: What is the problem? • Resolution: How is the problem solved? • Sequence of events: What was the order in which each main event happened?
Analyzes the characters.	Can't tell you or can't write anything about the characters.	Give your child a list of character traits. You might have to give him some examples. Have him choose between two and five traits that fit the character. Then he should tell you why he has chosen each trait.
Summarizes the text.	Wants to completely retell the whole story.	Tell your child you only want to know the setting and the main things that happened to the main characters.

time to bond with your child. You should also encourage him to read aloud to you from familiar books. This will help increase his reading rate (speed), comprehension, and confidence.

Increasing your child's reading rate while making sure he fully understands what he reads is very important in third grade. Skills that help include making predictions, identifying parts of the story, analyzing the characters, and summarizing the text.

The table on page 53 describes some important skills related to comprehension, where children can run into problems, and what you can do to help them along.

Comprehension Activities

1 Missing Punctuation

TIME: 20–30 minutes

MATERIALS
- word processing program
- one of your child's favorite stories retyped, without any punctuation

Learning happens when: you have your child read the story aloud without punctuation. Ask him if the story makes sense. He will probably say no. Ask your child why he thinks the story didn't make sense. Then show your child the story with the punctuation. Read the story aloud and have him follow along. Ask, "What did I do when I came to a comma or a period? Did that help you understand the story?" Have your child read the story aloud with the punctuation to decide when to make the appropriate pauses and stops. Ask him if it makes a difference to his understanding.

Variations: Instead of having your child read aloud first, try reading the story to him without punctuation. It might be more efficient for your child to hear it first to get the idea of how funny it sounds. Choose a new story for him to read aloud and practice using the punctuation as cues for reading.

✍ Your kinesthetic learner might enjoy retyping the story without the punctuation.

👁 Have your visual learner draw or write the punctuation marks on a large sheet of paper. Then as he listens to the story, your child can point to the punctuation marks as he "hears" them being read. Your child could also make a tally mark for each type of punctuation that he hears, then tell you the totals at the end of each page or section or at the end of the story.

👂 Your auditory learner will enjoy reading aloud for the whole activity.

Mastery occurs when: your child can read the story using the punctuation as cues for when to pause and stop.

You may want to help your child a little more if: he can't read the story and make the correct pauses and stops. He will need to practice at phrasing the sentences for meaning or saying the words in the rhythm that conveys the meaning. A simple example is the word "pardon." You can say "pardon" (as you would say "excuse me"), or you can say "pardon?" (as you would say "what?"). Try to find a shorter passage for your child to practice this concept.

2 | Making Predictions

Learning happens when: your child uses her previous experiences to make predictions in a story. Before you begin to read your child's favorite book, have your child look at the cover of the book and the title and make predictions about what she thinks the book will be about. Ask your child what makes her think a certain event will happen. Also ask if something similar has ever

TIME: 20–30 minutes

MATERIALS
▫ a favorite book and/or a new book

happened to her. Have your child predict who the main character is and what she thinks the character will be like. Have your child read aloud one page of the book at a time, making predictions of what will happen on the next page. After each page, check to see if her predictions were correct. Continue until she has completed ten pages.

Variations: Ask your child to take turns with you reading one page at a time. Encourage her to make predictions along with you. Switch books, trying the same activity with a new book.

Ask your child to act out a few of her predictions.

Ask your visual learner to record her predictions and what really happened on a sheet of paper or a chart.

Your auditory learner will be very comfortable doing the activity as is.

Mastery occurs when: your child can use her previous experiences to make appropriate predictions.

You might want to help you child a little more if: her predictions do not make sense or relate to the story at all. You can make your own predictions as a model for your child. The more your child hears appropriate predictions, the better she will be at making her own.

3 Sequencing Main Event Plates

Learning happens when: you and your child brainstorm the events that happened in a book he has recently read. Write only one event on each index card, choosing six to eight of the most important events in the story. Ask your child to place the events (cards) in the order they happened in the story. Then have him draw lines to divide the paper plate into six to eight equal parts (however many main events he decided upon). When your child has divided the plate into sections, he should draw and color pictures to represent each event in the story in each part of the paper plate. On the back of the plate, he should copy the sentences describing the main events that he wrote on the index cards in sequential order.

Variations: Let your child decide how to divide the paper plate into parts. He might decide that one event is a lot more important to the story than the other events, so this event should take up a bigger space on the plate to emphasize its importance.

TIME: 20–30 minutes

MATERIALS
- recently read book
- pencils
- index cards
- paper plate (the cheap, thin kind is best)
- colored pencils

- This activity is especially good for your kinesthetic learner because he is active during most of the project manipulating the index cards as well as drawing and coloring.

- This activity is great for your visual learner because he not only puts the concepts into writing but also into pictures.

- Ask your child to retell the story to you using the paper plate as an aid.

Mastery occurs when: your child is able to select the six to eight most important events and explain his choices. Your child should also be able to place the events in the correct order of occurrence.

You might want to help your child a little more if: he is having trouble identifying the most important events. Discuss the story with him. Help choose the first major event in the story and explain why it is important. Then give your child a choice for the next major event. This will narrow the choices and make it a little easier. You might try an easier or more familiar story for the first couple of times you complete the activity.

4 | Identifying Parts of a Story

TIME: 20–30 minutes

MATERIALS

■ paper
■ pencils
■ recently read book (the first time you do this activity, choose a short, interesting book you have read together)

Photocopy the following graphic organizer or type it on a computer.

Title of Book	
Setting	
Main Characters Name and a short description	1. 2. 3.
Main Conflict	
Main Events in Sequence	1. 2. 3. 4. 5. 6.
Resolution How was the conflict solved?	

Learning happens when: you and your child read the book, then discuss and fill in the information about the story on the graphic organizer.

Variations: Have your child do the activity on her own rather than with you. Before she begins, you might want to brainstorm a list of the main events that happened in the story. Then she can evaluate or choose which events were the most important. Once your child has chosen the main events, she should put them in the correct sequence.

- Your kinesthetic learner will like brainstorming and writing the events on individual index cards so that she can place them in the correct sequence.

- Your visual learner might also want to have a space on the graphic organizer to draw and color a small picture to go with the information.

- Ask your child to present the information to you in a news report. She can also record it onto a tape.

Mastery occurs when: your child can identify and describe all the parts of the story.

You might want to help your child a little more if: she is having trouble identifying some parts of the story. Find out which parts she does not understand, then reread those parts with her. Help her describe them. Give your child a chance to identify another part of the story, with you guiding her by asking questions related to that part.

5 Character Web

TIME: 30–40 minutes

MATERIALS
- recently read book
- paper
- pencils

Learning happens when: you re-read the story with your child and he draws a picture of the main character in the center of the paper. Have him draw three or four circles or ovals around the picture and connect these to the picture with lines. Brainstorm a list of character traits—for example, friendly, respectful, serious, and trusting. (You can find a list of character traits at www.knowledgeessentials.com.) Have your child choose three or four traits belonging to the main character in the story and write one in each oval or circle. Then have him draw a box coming off of each circle and describe how the character used that trait in the story.

Variations: Ask your child to draw a picture of the event in each box that shows how the character used that trait.

- Ask your kinesthetic learner to act out the part in each of the boxes to bring added meaning to them.

- This activity is great for your visual learner because the whole thing is done as a visual aid. He could add color to help distinguish different character traits.

- Ask your child to give an oral report on the character. It could be in the form of an announcement about an award the character might receive because of his traits.

Mastery occurs when: your child can identify character traits and choose examples to show how the character has demonstrated those traits.

You may want to help your child a little more if: he can't identify three or four character traits or pick an example of how the character used those traits. You might have to give him hints or a choice between two traits or events to help him get the idea.

6 | Create Your Own Titles

Copy the following graphic organizer by hand or type it on a computer:

TIME: 20–30 minutes

MATERIALS
recently read book
without chapter titles
paper
pencils

Title of Book:	
Chapter	**Chapter Title**
1	
2	
3	
4	
5	
6	
7	
8	

Learning happens when: your child brainstorms a list of titles for each chapter in the book you chose. Then your child selects the title she believes is best for each chapter and writes the names for each chapter in the graphic organizer.

- Ask your child to act out a short scene that demonstrates why she chose each particular title.
- Ask your child to draw a small picture to go with each chapter title.
- Using the chapter titles as a reminder of what happened in the story, ask your child to briefly retell the story.

Mastery occurs when: your child can give you a reasonable explanation for the titles she chose for each chapter.

You may want to help your child a little more if: she gives unreasonable titles to the chapters. Reread each chapter with her and discuss the main events in that chapter. Decide on a title for the first couple of chapters together. If your child is still having difficulty, you might want to switch to a book that is written on an easier level.

7 | Short Summary

TIME: 20–30 minutes

MATERIALS
- short, simple newspaper article
- paper
- pencils

Learning happens when: you have your child read the newspaper article and write short answers to the following questions:

Title of Article:

Who?

What?

Where?

When?

Why?

When your child has finished answering these questions, ask him to write a short summary of the article in complete sentences.

Variations: Your child can use these same questions to write a summary of each chapter in a book.

 If your child is a kinesthetic learner, ask him to use a highlighter as he reads the article to highlight the parts that answer the questions.

👁 Your visual learner can draw small pictures to go with the answer to each question.

🕪 Encourage your child to read the answers to the questions aloud to you. He can also dictate the summary to you while you write it down for him. Then ask him to read the summary back to you.

Mastery occurs when: your child can accurately answer the questions and write a summary containing the main facts in the article.

You might want to help your child a little more if: he can't answer the questions about the article. You can help him use a highlighter to mark the information that will answer the questions.

8 Puppet Show

Rewrite on a sheet of paper the table on page 64 or print it from www.knowledgeessentials.com.

Learning happens when: your child identifies the setting, main characters, and events from a story she has read. She will then make sock puppets of a few of the characters. Have your child use details from the story to make the characters look similar to the characters described in the book. Your child should then create a storyboard of scenes from the story in sequential order using the table you made. She should draw a picture and write a short script for each scene. Once the script and puppets are ready, have your child practice the puppet show until she feels comfortable enough to perform it for you.

Variations: You can get as elaborate as you want. You can make a theater out of a large box and create different scenery as needed. The scenery can be drawn and colored on large pieces of paper and attached to the back of the box.

TIME: 50–60 minutes

MATERIALS
- previously read book
- paper
- pencils
- old, clean socks
- yarn
- buttons
- thread
- sewing needles

Your child will enjoy this project because she will get to move around a lot and use her hands to make the puppets.

Your visual learner will benefit because the storyboard and the actual presentation are visual.

Acting out the different scenes will help your child easily grasp the meaning and parts of the story.

Mastery occurs when: your child successfully completes the presentation of the puppet show.

You may want to help your child a little more if: she seems to get frustrated at any step during the activity. Get your child through the problem areas by giving her a hint or doing part of the activity as an example. You might make it a family activity and share the responsibilities.

Scene 1	Scene 2	Scene 3	Scene 4	Scene 5
Scene 6	Scene 7	Scene 8	Scene 9	Scene 10

Environmental Learning

Your child will be able to use her life experiences to relate to literature and participate in discussions. The more different experiences your child has, the better able she will be to make connections to literature and to comprehend what she is reading. Take her to different places, such as museums, zoos, and vacation spots. Get her involved in some activities she enjoys, such as sports, dance, art, or a chess club.

Make reading the newspaper a daily activity with your child. There is always something to discuss with her. It could be in the world, state, or local news, or in the sports, entertainment, or even the comics section.

Be sure your child has the opportunity to practice reading just as she would practice a sport or a musical instrument.

End of Third Grade Reading Checklist

Students who are working at the standard level at the end of third grade:

_____ Read with understanding and fluency

_____ Understand the meaning of synonyms, homonyms, and antonyms

_____ Can identify the meanings of compound words

_____ Use punctuation cues to add meaning to the text

_____ Use graphic organizers to aid comprehension

_____ Make reasonable predictions

_____ Identify the main ideas of passages

_____ Can identify character traits

_____ Summarize what they have read

_____ Have a larger sight vocabulary

Third Grade Writing 6

In third grade, writing becomes more complicated. Not only will your child be writing book reports, he will learn to do research papers. Writing is now an important activity in every subject area. Your child must learn to use his writing skills in new ways.

Third grade students finally get to learn how to write in cursive, which most kids think is great. They feel like they're finally big kids. Third graders are asked to respond in writing in almost every subject, even math, so they need to know how to write their thoughts and ideas. Third graders will continue to focus on the parts of speech and how to use them to make their writing more interesting.

> ## Beginning of Third Grade Writing Checklist
>
> Students who are working at the standard level at the beginning of third grade:
>
> _____ Write about their own ideas
>
> _____ Pick out nouns and verbs in sentences
>
> _____ Explain the problem, solution, and main idea in fiction and nonfiction
>
> _____ Revise their writing to make it clearer
>
> _____ Read and understand stories, poems, plays, directories, newspapers, charts, and diagrams
>
> _____ Write different types of sentences

Cursive Handwriting

Now that your child can print well, it is time for her to learn cursive writing. Why do we learn to write in two ways? The point of cursive is that all of the letters are connected so that you never have to lift your pencil off the paper. Cursive is a more efficient, faster way of writing; printing is easier to read.

Learning cursive is harder than you may remember. Your child will need to be able to identify the letter to be written, use memory to recall what the letter should look like in cursive, then hold the mental picture of the letter while forming it on paper.

There are several ways to introduce and reinforce cursive writing that take some of the pressure off your child. One example is to use your finger as the pencil and draw the letters in a sandbox or in a cake pan filled with salt. Or you can draw the letters with your finger in the air. Your child will need to practice, practice, practice. She will improve as she works on individual letter formation, then as she practices blending the letters together into words. The table below describes some important skills related to handwriting, where children can run into problems, and what you can do to help them along.

Now that you have an idea of the mechanics of cursive writing as well as what to expect, let's look at some activities to enhance these skills.

Cursive Handwriting Skills	Having Problems?	Quick Tips
Copies easily from the board, overhead, book, or paper.	Has difficulty copying from the board, overhead, book, or paper.	Ask your child to trace and then copy from a piece of paper on his desk.
Writes legibly and consistently forms letters in cursive.	Cursive writing not legible and letter formation inconsistent.	Employ alternate writing strategies such as tracing on a transparency over another piece of writing.
Writes cursive letters quickly and easily.	Has difficulty writing cursive letters quickly and easily.	Practice, practice, practice!
Holds pen or pencil comfortably.	Has an awkward or uncomfortable grip on the pen or pencil.	What may be awkward or uncomfortable to you may not be to your child. If she persists in holding a pencil in a certain way, it may be wise to let her.

Cursive Handwriting Activities

1 Cursive Word Shapes

Have you ever noticed that if you outline familiar words the shape of the outline looks familiar, too? You will need to write out a list of words that are familiar to your child in lowercase cursive letters on the chart paper. Then draw an outline around the words. Use the outline as a pattern by cutting it out and tracing around it, or you can erase the word inside the shape you just drew. On either the chart paper or a sheet of plain paper, create two columns: one for the words and one for their shapes.

Learning happens when: you explain to your child that individual letters make up words, but the word itself also has its own shape (design). Ask your child to match the word to its shape by drawing a line between the word and the shape. Then write the letters that make the design inside the shape. Check and correct as needed. After the matching is finished, ask your child to write the words in cursive as you say them. If your child has trouble with this, ask him to find the shape of the first letter on the alphabet chart, then use that letter to help guess the word. Keep a list of these words and their shapes in a folder for future reference.

Variations: Choose other common words to use in the future. You might try cutting the shapes of the words into pieces and have your child put them together like a puzzle. After the pieces have been put together, your child can trace the shape, then write the word in cursive inside the traced shape.

Your kinesthetic learner may enjoy tracing the word shapes and setting the activity up with you.

TIME: 30 minutes

MATERIALS
- colored pencils
- chart paper
- cursive alphabet chart (many educational supply stores sell strips that have the alphabet printed on them in both uppercase and lowercase cursive letters; if you can't find one, go to www.knowledge essentials.com to find examples of cursive letters)
- rounded-edge scissors

- 👁 Visual learners will like the variation of this activity where the shapes are cut into puzzle pieces. They will enjoy recognizing shape patterns and matching them to the shape of the words.

- 👂 Ask your auditory learner to say the words aloud as they are matched to their shapes in order to reinforce learning.

Mastery occurs when: your child can match the shapes of the words to the words written in cursive and can write the words correctly in cursive.

You may want to help your child a little more if: he is having problems matching the words to their shapes. You may want to narrow the choices for matching. You might try writing the word yourself, then having your child trace it.

2 Alphabet Shakeup

Learning happens when: you and your child cut each index card into eight pieces. Then have your child use the markers to write one cursive lowercase letter on each card until you have one of every letter of the alphabet. Put the completed cards in a small container and shake them up. Give your child some cursive paper and a pencil. Have her pick a cursive letter out of the container, then copy it onto the cursive paper. She can look at the alphabet chart if she needs help remembering the shapes of the letters. Continue until your child has written all of the letters.

Variations: Try putting only uppercase letters or both types of letters in the container.

 Try setting up a marker board at one end of the room for your kinesthetic learner. When your child pulls a letter out of the container, she can run to the other side of the room and copy the letter on the marker board. Remind her that the correct form and neatness of the letters count.

👁 This activity is good for your visual learner because there is a visual cue for each letter of the alphabet on the cards. Another idea would be to ask your child to trace the letter she made the first time with a colored pencil.

👂 Ask your aural learner to say the letter name when she picks the letter from the container and repeat the letter name when she writes it.

Mastery occurs when: your child can successfully copy each letter of the alphabet in cursive.

You may want to help your child a little more if: she is not able to copy the letters of the alphabet in cursive. You could reduce the amount of letters in the container. You might group the letters into categories by something that is similar in the making of each letter, such as a straight line in *b* or *p.* Have your child practice the small groups of letters until she is successful with them, then work on a new group of letters.

3 Blending Letters

Learning happens when: you and your child cut each index card into eight pieces. Then have your child use the markers to write one cursive lowercase letter on each card until you have one of every letter of the alphabet. Put the completed cards in a small container and shake them up. Give your child some cursive paper and a pencil. Have him pick eight to ten letters out of the container (making sure there are at least one or two vowels), then

TIME: 20–30 minutes

MATERIALS
- rounded-edge scissors
- 4 index cards
- markers
- small container
- cursive paper (available at stores that sell school supplies, or you can print some out from www .knowledgeessentials.com)
- pencils
- cursive alphabet chart (many educational supply stores sell strips that have the alphabet printed on them in both uppercase and lowercase cursive letters; if you can't find one, go to www .knowledgeessentials.com to find examples of cursive letters)

TIME: 20–30 minutes

MATERIALS
- rounded-edge scissors
- 4 index cards
- markers
- small container
- cursive paper (available at stores that sell school supplies, or you can print some out from www .knowledgeessentials.com)
- pencils
- cursive alphabet chart (many educational supply stores sell strips that have the alphabet printed on them in both uppercase and lowercase cursive letters; if you can't find one, go to www .knowledgeessentials.com to find examples of cursive letters)

place these letter cards on a table with the letters facing up. He should try to spell a word with some or all of these letters. Have him copy the word in cursive on the cursive paper.

Variations: To make sure your child draws a few vowels, try writing the vowel cursive letters on index cards that are a different color than the consonant cards. Try asking your child to make several words with the same group of letters.

✋ Your child will learn well with this activity because he is manipulating the letter cards into words.

👁 Your visual learner will do well because he will be able to see the letters forming the words before he writes them.

👂 Ask your aural learner to say the letter names as he chooses the correct letters for a word. When your child has completed writing the word, ask him to say it aloud.

Mastery occurs when: your child can successfully make words from the cursive letters and copy the words onto paper.

You may want to help your child a little more if: he is having trouble making a word with the letters or can't successfully write the word in cursive. If your child can't make a word from the letters, you might give him a hint, such as a beginning letter of a possible word. If he is having trouble writing the word in cursive, you can copy the word in cursive yourself, then have your child trace it several times in different colors with colored pencils.

4 Sentence Building

Learning happens when: you and your child cut each index card into eight pieces. Then have your child use the markers to write a word from the list in cursive on each card. Put the completed cards in a small container and shake them up. Give your child some cursive paper and a pencil. Have her pick about a dozen words from the container. Then ask her to try to make a sentence out of the words. If she can't make a complete sentence, have her draw another word card, then try to make a sentence. When your child has made a sentence with the cards, have her copy the sentence in cursive onto the paper.

Variations: Try using different-colored index cards for different parts of speech. That way it will be easier to make sentences because you can be sure your child has the parts of speech she needs. Challenge your child to see if she can make a sentence using all of the words that have been drawn.

- This is a good activity for your kinesthetic learner because she will be moving as she is drawing the cards and manipulating them into sentences.

- This activity is good for your visual learner because she sees the word written in cursive on the card.

- Ask your aural learner to say each word as it is drawn from the container. When all of the cards have been drawn and read aloud, she can use the words to make a sentence. Read the sentence aloud, then ask your child to repeat the sentence before she writes it.

Mastery occurs when: your child can use the words to form a sentence and write the complete sentence in cursive.

TIME: 20–30 minutes

MATERIALS
- rounded-edge scissors
- 4 index cards
- list of words (from your child's school spelling list plus familiar verbs, nouns, adjectives, and adverbs for variety; you can find some sample word lists for this activity at www.knowledge essentials.com)
- markers
- small container
- cursive paper (available at stores that sell school supplies, or you can print some out from www .knowledgeessentials.com)
- pencils
- cursive alphabet chart (many educational supply stores sell strips that have the alphabet printed on them in both uppercase and lowercase cursive letters; if you can't find one, go to www .knowledgeessentials.com to find examples of cursive letters)

You may want to help your child a little more if: she is not able to make a sentence with the words or if she can't copy the words correctly in cursive. If your child can't make a sentence from the words, give her a hint or the beginning word of a possible sentence. If your child can't copy the sentence correctly, copy the sentence yourself as she watches, then have her trace the sentence with a colored pencil.

5 | Poetry

TIME: 20–30 minutes

MATERIALS

▪ poetry book (Shel Silverstein's works are good for this activity)

▪ pencils

▪ cursive paper (available at stores that sell school supplies, or you can print some out from www .knowledgeessentials.com)

▪ cursive alphabet chart (many educational supply stores sell strips that have the alphabet printed on them in both uppercase and lowercase cursive letters; if you can't find one, go to www.knowledge essentials.com to find examples of cursive letters)

Learning happens when: your child chooses a poem and copies it in cursive on the cursive paper. Your child can use the cursive alphabet chart to remind him of how to form each letter.

Variations: your child can make up his own poem to write in cursive.

Ask your kinesthetic learner to practice writing each word or sentence with his finger in a shallow container with a layer of salt or rice on the bottom. Then he could write the word or sentence on the cursive paper.

Try writing the poem in cursive yourself for your child to use as a guide for his own writing.

Encourage your child to say each letter aloud as he writes it on the cursive paper. Then let him read the whole poem aloud.

Mastery occurs when: your child can copy the poem in cursive correctly and easily.

You may want to help your child a little more if: he is having difficulty forming the letters and writing the words. Try practicing one word at a time until he is comfortable with each word. You might try writing the word yourself, then having your child trace over your word.

Grammar

Writing sentences and paragraphs requires your child to remember several things simultaneously (forming letters and words, using correct grammar and punctuation, and recalling the ideas he wants to write). If a child has a hard time retrieving any of this information from long- or short-term memory, the entire writing process will be more difficult.

Some new aspects of grammar are introduced in third grade, such as the basic parts of speech and sentence structure. They are practiced continuously as your child goes through school. Third graders also learn the different types of sentences. See the sidebar on page 76 for a refresher on what your third grader is learning. You can refer to it as you're doing some of the activities.

The following table describes some important skills related to comprehension, where children run into problems, and what you can do to help them along.

Grammar Skills	Having Problems?	Quick Tips
Identifies nouns.	Can't identify all the nouns in a sentence.	Nouns name a person, place, thing, or idea. Ask who? or what? as you practice with your child.
Identifies verbs.	Can't identify all of the verbs in a sentence.	Ask your child what the subject is doing as you practice with your child.
Identifies adjectives.	Can't identify all of the adjectives in a sentence.	Tell your child that adjectives describe nouns. Ask what kind? and how many? as you practice with your child.
Identifies adverbs.	Can't identify all of the adverbs in a sentence.	Adverbs tell about the verbs, adjective, or another adverb in a sentence. They answer when? where? why? and under what conditions? Adverbs frequently end in "ly."

Basic Grammar Concepts

Helping your child grapple with grammar can get confusing, so let's take a look at two grammar concepts that you should be prepared to help your child with, now and for the next ten years: the basic parts of speech and sentence fundamentals.

The Basic Parts of Speech

adjective A word that modifies a noun; it describes a quality of a person, place, or thing.

adverb A word that describes a verb, an adjective, or another adverb; it often ends in *ly*.

conjunction "Junction what's your function? Hookin' up words and phrases and clauses." As the classic *Schoolhouse Rock* song tells us, conjunctions are words such as "and," "or," and "but" that connect words, ideas, phrases, clauses, and sentences into one big sentence or idea.

interjection An exclamation or utterance such as "wow," "oh," or "huh."

noun Names a person, place, thing, feeling, idea, or act.

plural noun Refers to two or more people, places, or things.

proper noun Names a particular person (someone's name), place, or thing and begins with a capital letter.

preposition Shows the relationship between one noun and a different noun, verb, or adverb, such as "in" or "through."

pronoun Replaces a noun, such as "he," "they," or "it."

singular noun Refers to one person, place, or thing.

verb Describes action.

verb tense Tells you when the action happened. The main forms are present (I sing), past (I sang), future (I will sing), present participle (I am singing), and past participle (I have sung).

Sentence Fundamentals

What makes a sentence? For a group of words to be a sentence it needs three things:

1. The words make sense and express a complete thought.

2. It begins with a capital letter and ends with a period, exclamation point, or question mark.

3. It contains a predicate and a subject. The predicate, or verb, tells what the subject, or noun, is doing.

Sentences can be any length, as long as they follow these rules.

The parts of a sentence include:

direct object   A noun or pronoun that is having an action done to it.

indirect object   A noun or pronoun that tells you for what or whom the action of the verb (predicate) is being done.

predicate   The verb that describes what the noun (subject) of the sentence is doing or being.

subject   A noun or pronoun that is performing the verb; the "doer" of a sentence.

The following are examples of subject and predicate:

1. Brittany runs the mile.

    Brittany is the subject; *runs* is the predicate; *mile* is the direct object.

2. Matt threw Luke the football.

    Matt is the subject; *threw* is the predicate; *Luke* is the indirect object; *football* is the direct object.

A **compound sentence** is two sentences joined together using a conjunction. The most common conjunctions are "and," "although," "as," "because," "but," "if," "or," "though," "where," and "whether." Conjunctions that indicate time are: "before," "after," "until," "since," "when," "whenever," and "while."

The following sentences show how conjunctions are used:

Amy sold the blue coat *and* it was dirty.

Amy sold the blue coat *because* it was dirty.

Amy sold the blue coat *before* it was dirty.

Notice how the conjunctions change the meaning of the sentence, so choosing the right one is important!

Types of Sentences

declarative   A sentence that makes a statement. A declarative sentence ends with a period.

Example: Marcus is a basketball player

(continued)

imperative   A sentence that is a command. An imperative sentence ends in a period. The subject of an imperative sentence is always understood to be you, even though "you" is not stated in the sentence.

Examples: Shut the door. Go to bed. Wash the dishes.

exclamatory   A sentence that expresses strong feelings or emotions. An exclamatory sentence ends in an exclamation point.

Examples: We won the game! Ow, that hurt!

interrogative   A sentence that asks a question. An interrogative sentence ends in a question mark.

Examples: Do you want to go to the park? What are we having for dinner?

Try some of these activities to help your child practice what he is learning at school.

Grammar Activities

 ABC Book of Nouns

TIME: 20–30 minutes

MATERIALS
- paper
- pencils
- stapler
- colored pencils

Learning happens when: your child brainstorms a list of three to five nouns for each letter of the alphabet. Have your child fold eight sheets of paper in half to form a book. Staple the pages together at the fold in the middle of the book. The book should include a cover and one page for each letter of the alphabet. Your child should write the nouns he has chosen on the appropriate alphabet page (e.g., "a" for "apple"). He should draw and color an illustration for each noun.

Variations: Include a sentence for each noun. Make the sentences tell a story throughout the entire book. Try the activity with verbs, adjectives, and adverbs.

✋ Ask your child to cut illustrations out of construction paper or a magazine and glue them into the book.

👁 Your child will enjoy drawing an illustration to go with each noun, and it will help humor him to remember the words.

👂 Encourage your child to read each page aloud as he is creating the book, then reread it when the book is completed.

Mastery occurs when: your child can identify three to five nouns for each letter of the alphabet.

You may want to help your child a little more if: he is having trouble identifying nouns for each letter of the alphabet. Try doing the book with only one noun on each page. Later on, your child can go back and identify more nouns for each letter.

2 Describing Me

Learning happens when: your child draws a picture of herself on a large piece of paper and colors it. Then she should brainstorm a list of twenty adjectives that describe herself. From that list your child should choose about a dozen adjectives that best describe her and write the words on the paper around the picture.

Variations: At the bottom of the paper your child can write three to five sentences about herself using the adjectives.

✋ Ask your child to find the adjectives to describe herself in a newspaper or magazine. She should cut the adjectives out and glue them onto the paper around the picture.

👁 Ask your visual learner to draw and color nouns that could be described by the adjectives (e.g., blue box, red car, etc.).

👂 Ask your child to read her adjectives aloud.

TIME: 20–30 minutes

MATERIALS
large sheet of paper
colored pencils
pencils

Mastery occurs when: your child can identify adjectives to describe herself.

You may want to help your child a little more if: she can't describe herself with adjectives. Try asking: What kind of things do you like? How many brothers, sisters, or cousins do you have? Which one of the cartoons is your favorite?

3 Snap It and Clap It

TIME: 10 minutes

MATERIALS
list of short sentences

Learning happens when: you tell your child you are going to read a sentence aloud. When you say a word that is an adjective, your child is going to snap his fingers. When you say a word that is an adverb, your child is going to clap his hands. Read the sentences and watch to see if he does the correct movement.

Variations: Let your child choose the movement he wants to do for each part of speech. Add other movements for other parts of speech.

You will not need to change anything about this activity for your kinesthetic child as it already involves movement.

Ask your child to look at the sentences first. Encourage him to underline the adjectives and circle the adverbs in each sentence. Then read the sentences aloud and ask him to perform the appropriate movement for each part of speech.

Ask your child to read the sentence aloud first. Then you can reread the sentence to your child and ask him to perform the appropriate movement for each part of speech.

Mastery occurs when: your child can make the right movement as he hears the adverbs and adjectives.

You may want to help your child a little more if: he is not making the correct movement for the adjectives and adverbs. Try focusing on one part of speech at a time. Also try writing the sentence on a dry erase board so that he can see the words as you read the sentence.

4 | Types of Sentences

Write each of the following words on a large piece of paper: "Declarative," "Imperative," "Interrogative," and "Exclamatory." Also put these end marks on separate pieces of paper: !, ., ?.

TIME: 20–30 minutes

MATERIALS

paper

pencils

list of various types of sentences

Learning happens when: you give the pieces of paper to your child, then read a sentence to her. She should hold up the piece of paper with the correct type of sentence written on it and the piece of paper with the correct end mark on it.

Variations: Your child can make up her own sentences.

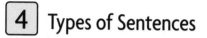 Your kinesthetic learner will learn well from this activity as it is.

Try writing the sentences down for your visual learner to see.

Write the sentences down and ask your child to read them aloud before you do the activity.

Mastery occurs when: your child can correctly identify the type of sentence and the correct end punctuation.

You may want to help your child a little more if: she can't correctly identify the type of sentence or punctuation. Try focusing on just two choices of the types of sentences. For example, use only declarative and interrogative sentences. Once your child is comfortable with these, add another type of sentence to her choices.

5 What I Do!

TIME: 20–30 minutes
(over a week or so)

MATERIALS
- journal
- pencils

Learning happens when: your child keeps a journal of things he has done for each day of one week, using only compound sentences. For example: On Monday I went to the store, and I bought a new shirt. After the week is over, have your child read the entries.

Variations: Your child can write compound sentences that combine activities from more than one of the days of the week. Ask him to look for patterns. Is there something that he did every day of the week?

- Your kinesthetic learner can use the computer to keep his journal.

- Ask your child to make notes of the things he did each day. Then he can use the notes as a visual aid to write the compound sentences. The notes might help him decide which conjunction to use in the compound sentence.

- Ask your child to read the compound sentences aloud.

Mastery occurs when: your child can write a compound sentence using the correct conjunction.

You may want to help your child a little more if: he can't write a compound sentence or use the correct conjunction. Try starting the sentence for your child and letting him finish it. You could also tell him what conjunction to use for the sentence.

Spelling

As your child gets older, the spelling words become longer and harder. Children can use their phonics lessons to sound out the words, but this doesn't always help to spell them correctly. Your child will also learn all kinds of rules for how to spell words. But rules are made to be broken, and just as your child learns a new rule, along comes a word that breaks the rule. Your child will also learn how to break words into syllables to help spell them more easily. The following table describes an important skill related to spelling, where children run into problems, and what you can do to help them along.

Spelling Skills	Having Problems?	Quick Tips
Correctly spells most words when writing.	Frequently misspells words while writing.	Use flash cards and go over common spelling rules, such as *i* before *e* except after *c.*

Spelling Activities

1 Erase Away

Write a spelling word on the dry erase board. Add one or a few extra letters to the word that shouldn't be there. For example, if the spelling word is "wheel," you could write the word "wheele."

Learning happens when: you tell your child what the word is, then have him repeat the word aloud and erase the letter(s) that shouldn't be there.

Variations: Try writing the vowels in one color and the consonants in another color. Your child can try writing the word correctly below the original spelling before erasing the extra letters.

 Your kinesthetic learner will learn well with the activity just the way it is because he is actively erasing the letters that aren't needed.

TIME: 20–30 minutes

MATERIALS
- dry erase board
- dry erase markers
- list of spelling words (use your child's school spelling words or go to www.knowledge essentials.com for suggestions)

- 👁 Ask your child to rewrite the word below the original to help him decide which letters need to be erased.

- 👂 Ask your child to spell the word aloud as he decides what letters need to be erased.

Mastery occurs when: your child can choose the correct letters to be erased.

You may want to help your child a little more if: he can't figure out which letters do not belong in the word. Try saying the word slowly to your child to see if he can hear the letter sounds. Break the word into syllables and repeat the word. You might have to tell your child which syllable(s) the extra letter(s) is in.

2 | Making Words

Time: 20–30 minutes

Materials
- list of spelling words (use your child's school spelling words or go to www.knowledge essentials.com for suggestions)
- paper
- pencils
- rounded-edge scissors
- index cards

Write the letters of a word in alphabetical order, putting the vowels first, then the consonants. For example, for the word "basketball" the letters would be in this order: a a e b b k l l s t.

Learning happens when: you have your child see how many words she can make from these letters. Tell her that there is a big word that uses all of the letters. Have your child cut the index cards into squares and write one letter from the word on each square. She can now manipulate the letter squares to form words. Each time she makes a new word, she should write it down on paper.

Variations: Instead of putting the letters on index cards, you could buy magnetic letters and let your child manipulate them into words on the refrigerator or a baking sheet. After your child has made a lot of words, see if she can organize the words into categories using common spelling patterns. For example, one category could be words with a long *a* sound while another category might be words that end with a consonant-e combination.

Your child will do well with the activity in the original version or the variation because she will learn well by manipulating the letters.

👁 This activity is good for your visual learner because she is able to see if each word looks right.

👂 Ask your child to say each letter as she is spelling a word. When she finishes a word, have her say it aloud.

Mastery occurs when: your child can correctly spell several words from the letters, including the big word.

You may want to help your child a little more if: she seems to be having trouble spelling words from the letters. Try giving your child a hint by providing a pattern where she needs to change only the beginning letter(s) to make a new word.

3 Roll the Dice

Draw lines on the chart paper or dry erase board to indicate spaces for the letters of one of the spelling words.

Learning happens when: your child rolls the dice and guesses a consonant. If he chooses one of the letters that is in the word, he gets the amount of points rolled on the dice. For example, if a 7 was rolled and the letter guessed appeared twice in the word, your child would get 14 points. The points are added together each time your child makes a correct guess. If he wants to guess a vowel, it will cost the amount of points rolled on the dice. When a correct letter is guessed, write the letters on the chart paper or dry erase board in the correct space.

Variations: You can play the game as a competition between you and your child or between two children. Players should each take

> **TIME:** 20–30 minutes
>
> **MATERIALS**
> ▪ chart paper or dry erase board
> ▪ pencils or dry erase markers
> ▪ list of spelling words (use your child's school spelling words or go to www.knowledge essentials.com for suggestions)
> ▪ 2 dice

a turn, but they should have different spelling words with the same number of letters. The player with the most points at the end of the game wins.

- ✋ Your kinesthetic learner will enjoy this activity as it is because there is a lot of movement.

- 👁 If your child is a visual learner, he will also do well with this activity as it is written because he will be able to see the letters going up on the board.

- 👂 Ask your child to say the letters in order, including the blanks, when it is his turn. This will help him figure out the next letter to choose.

Mastery occurs when: your child guesses appropriate letters and figures out the correct word.

You may want to help your child a little more if: he guesses letters that don't seem appropriate or can't figure out the correct word. Try giving him a hint or choose words that have a common spelling pattern.

4 My Spelling Story

TIME: 20–30 minutes

MATERIALS
- list of spelling words (use your child's school spelling words or go to www.knowledge essentials.com for suggestions)
- paper
- pencils

Learning happens when: your child uses all of the spelling words from the list to write a story that makes sense. Have her read the story to you and discuss the plot. Have your child illustrate the story.

Variations: Try asking your child to write a poem instead of a story. She could also write a letter or a journal entry.

- ✋ Encourage your child to act out the story for you and the family. She might need to recruit a few actors.

👁 Your child will enjoy illustrating the story.

👂 Encourage your child to read the story to you dramatically or act it out.

Mastery occurs when: your child can use the spelling words correctly in a story.

You may want to help your child a little more if: the story doesn't make sense. Try giving her a story starter and ask questions to help organize the story.

5 | Salt Tray Spelling

Spread out a layer of salt in the bottom of a pan.

Learning happens when: you say each word to your child and he spells it in the salt with his finger.

Variations: You could also use rice or sugar.

✋ Your child will enjoy feeling the texture of the salt as he writes the word.

👁 Your child will learn better by seeing the word as it is written in the salt.

👂 Ask your child to say each letter as he is writing the word in the salt.

Mastery occurs when: your child can correctly spell the words from the spelling list.

You may want to help your child a little more if: he is not able to spell the words correctly. Try giving a hint, such as the beginning or ending sound.

TIME: 20–30 minutes

MATERIALS
- salt
- large pan
- list of spelling words (use your child's school spelling words or go to www.knowledge essentials.com for suggestions)

Glue Spelling

TIME: 20–30 minutes

MATERIALS
▪ list of spelling words
(use your child's school
spelling words or go
to www.knowledge
essentials.com for
suggestions)
▪ nontoxic glue
▪ construction paper
▪ rounded-edge scissors

Learning happens when: your child spells the words in glue on the construction paper. Let the glue dry, then cut the words out of the construction paper. Have your child close her eyes. Place one of the glue words in front of her. Your child should use her fingers to feel the word, starting from the left and saying each letter as she feels it. After the last letter is said, then she should say the word.

Variations: You can also form the letters out of modeling clay or Play-Doh.

✋ This is a great activity for your kinesthetic learner because she is able to feel the texture of the glue as she reads the word.

👁 If your child learns visually, she will enjoy and learn from seeing the word when it's first written with the glue.

👂 Your auditory learner will learn by saying each letter and then the final word.

Mastery occurs when: your child can correctly spell and say each word on the spelling list.

You may want to help your child a little more if: she can't spell the word correctly. Try giving her a hint or let your child look at the word as she spells it.

 Spelling Pictures

Learning happens when: your child writes the spelling word and its definition on paper. Then he should draw a picture that accurately represents the word.

Variations: This activity can be done on the computer with a word processing program and the clip art that is commonly included with it. You can also find some clip art at www.knowledgeessentials.com.

TIME: 20–30 minutes

MATERIALS
list of spelling words (use your child's school spelling words or go to www.knowledge essentials.com for suggestions)
dictionary
paper
colored pencils

✋ Your kinesthetic learner would probably prefer to do this activity on the computer.

👁 Your visual learner can benefit from either variation because both incorporate illustrations.

👂 Ask your child to read the word and its definition aloud.

Mastery occurs when: your child can accurately draw or choose a picture that represents the meaning of the word.

You may want to help your child a little more if: he can't spell the word or find or draw a picture to represent the word. Give a suggestion or explain the meaning of the word in another way.

8 | Spelling Squares

Learning happens when: your child writes a spelling word on graph paper with one letter taking up one or two squares. If a letter has a part that is taller than the square, such as *b*, then the letter would take up two squares. If a letter has a part that is lower than the square, such as *p*, then the letter would also take up two squares. A wide letter, such as *w* or *m*, would also take up two squares. Once your child has written the words on the graph paper, she should lightly color the squares to see the shape of the word.

Variations: Have your child write the words in cursive.

TIME: 20–30 minutes

MATERIALS
list of spelling words (use your child's school spelling words or go to www.knowledge essentials.com for suggestions)
graph paper
colored pencils

✋ Your kinesthetic learner should do well with the activity as it is written. She can also trace around the squares to highlight the shape more.

👁 This activity appeals to your visual learner because she is able to see the shape of the word as well as the correct spelling.

👂 Ask your child to spell the word aloud as it is being written and read the word aloud after it is written.

Mastery occurs when: your child can correctly spell the words.

You may want to help your child a little more if: she can't spell the words correctly. Try breaking the words into syllables to see if she can identify the sounds.

Environmental Learning

Your child has a lot of opportunities to practice writing skills in the everyday world. He could keep a journal or diary to record his thoughts. Have your child help you with a shopping list. Play spelling games in the car as you are driving. As you pass a business, say the name and see if your child can spell the word. Help your child find a pen pal so that he has a great reason to write letters. It could even be a relative or close friend.

End of Third Grade Writing Checklist

Students who are working at the standard level at the end of third grade:

_____ Communicate in writing

_____ Use writing to inform others

_____ Use writing to persuade others

_____ Can identify nouns, verbs, adjectives, and adverbs in a sentence

_____ Use adjectives to describe things and enhance their writing

_____ Correctly use conjunctions

_____ Correctly use common spelling rules

_____ Identify sentence types

_____ Write compound sentences

Third Grade Math

7

Third grade math begins with a review of the concepts learned in second grade. Your child will then build on the concepts he already knows and will also be learning some new ones. Third grade is really a critical year, as it is the bridge from simple computation to more complex skills. Your child will learn the multiplication and division facts, which are very important because the concepts taught in fourth grade require a firm foundation in multiplication and division.

The math your child will learn this year can be divided into four broad categories: number operations, number sense and patterns, geometry and measurement, and probability and statistics.

Beginning of Third Grade Math Checklist

Students who are working at the standard level at the beginning of third grade:

_____ Add and subtract two- and three-digit numbers, both with and without regrouping

_____ Read and write whole numbers

_____ Can tell in which place each of the digits is located

_____ Count combinations of coins

_____ Tell time on the clock and calendar

_____ Can measure in many ways

_____ Can read a thermometer

_____ Recognize and create basic shapes

Number Operations

Your child began learning to add and subtract two- and three-digit numbers last year. This year she will build this skill with longer numbers. Your child will be adding and subtracting three- and four-digit numbers

Number Operations Skills	Having Problems?	Quick Tips
Can add four-digit numbers.	Does not understand how to regroup (carry).	Have your child work the problems on graph paper, with only one digit written in each box. When the sum for a column is a two-digit number, help your child split the number by carrying the tens digit to the neighboring column and putting the ones digit under the current column.
Can subtract four-digit numbers.	Does not understand how to regroup (borrow).	Have your child think of comparing the digits in each column with a scenario. The top number is the money in his pocket. The bottom number is the price of a desired object. Does your child have enough money in his pocket to buy the item? If not, your child must borrow from the neighbor. Thinking of borrowing in terms of money can help some students understand regrouping.
Learns the multiplication facts through the tens.	Is overwhelmed by learning so many facts.	Get a multiplication chart. Start slowly. Learn the easy facts first, such as 0, 1, 2, 5, and 10. As your child learns the facts, color them on the multiplication chart. Use the commutative model so that when your child learns 1×9, she will color 1×9 and 9×1 on the chart. Seeing the chart filled with color can be an incentive for many students.
Learns the basic division facts.	Has trouble relating to division.	Create fact families $5 \times 6 = 30$ $6 \times 5 = 30$ $30 \div 6 = 5$ $30 \div 5 = 6$ to show how multiplication and division are related. Turning a division fact into a multiplication sentence can help your child. For example, $16 \div 4 =$ $4 \times \underline{\ \ } = 16$
Estimates sums and differences.	Forgets to round the numbers before adding or subtracting.	Practice rounding so that it becomes second-nature. Also, remind your child to look for the key word "estimate" in the directions. If she sees that word, it means round the numbers before adding or subtracting.

as well as money amounts. She will also learn the basic multiplication facts through the tens, as well as the related division facts. Your child will be asked to estimate sums and differences by rounding the numbers before adding or subtracting them. The table on page 92 describes some important skills related to number operations, where children can run into problems, and what you can do to help them along.

Number Operations Activities

1 Triangular Flash Cards

Make a set of triangular flash cards for the numbers (or you can buy triangular flash cards at an educational supply store). To make the cards yourself, hold the index card vertically. Take the upper right corner and fold it down to the left until it reaches the opposite side of the card. Make a fold. It should look like a triangle on top of a rectangle.

TIME: 15–20 minutes

MATERIALS
- index cards
- rounded-edge scissors
- 2 markers, different colors

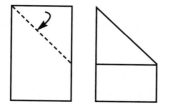

Cut off the bottom rectangle, which will leave the folded triangular portion. Open it up and cut across the fold so that you have two triangles.

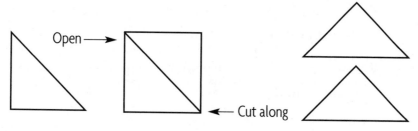

Open ⟶   ⟵ Cut along

Once you have several triangles, turn them so that the longest side is on the bottom, with the point upward. Your triangular flash cards have three corners, one at the top and two at the bottom. On the bottom corners, write the two numbers to be multiplied, using one marker color. On the top corner, write the answer, using a different marker color.

Learning happens when: you and your child practice these flash cards to learn the relationship between multiplication and division. Hold the flash cards so that your thumb is covering the top corner. Have your child multiply the bottom numbers. Remove your thumb to reveal the answer. Your child can do this on his own, receiving immediate feedback whether the answer was correct or incorrect.

Variations: Hold the flash cards so that one of the bottom corners is covered to review for the division facts. The top number is the dividend, and the bottom number is the divisor. The answer is the number under your thumb. The power of these triangular flash cards is that the relationship between multiplication and division is readily seen.

- Movers and shakers will probably prefer to use the flash cards themselves. It is more interesting for them.

- Your visual learner will benefit by the organization of the triangular flash cards. They help your child easily see the relationships between the numbers.

- If your child learns best by listening, have him say the entire fact instead of just the answer.

Mastery occurs when: your child can quickly say the facts and knows how multiplication and division are related.

You may want to help your child a little more if: he is feeling frustrated at the number of facts. Start with a smaller number of flash cards. Have your child experience more successes by learning a few facts at a time.

2 Multiplication War

Prepare the deck by removing the face cards. Make the aces equal to 1.

TIME: 10–15 minutes

MATERIALS
deck of cards

Learning happens when: you and your child play the multiplication version of the classic card game War. To play, deal the entire deck of cards between the two of you. You and your child should each flip over two cards at the same time. Then you each multiply your two cards together. The person with the greatest product wins all four cards. If someone gives an incorrect answer, the other person has to correctly multiply the two numbers to win all four cards. Play continues until all the cards have been played. The person with the greatest number of cards at the end of the game wins.

Variations: You and your child can compete directly with each other. Each person flips over one card, and you and your child simultaneously multiply the two numbers. The person who calls out the answer first wins both cards. If it is a tie, the two cards remain on the table and another pair of cards is flipped over. Whoever multiplies the new cards fastest wins all four cards.

- If your child likes to move, she will enjoy this game because she gets to flip the cards and gather them.

- Your visual learner may need a visual reminder to multiply. This can simply be an index card with the multiplication symbol on it.

*Ask your child to say the complete fact, rather than just the answer.

Mastery occurs when: your child successfully multiplies the numbers together.

You may want to help your child a little more if: she is having trouble multiplying the numbers. Make a rule such as "multiply by 2." Each of you flips only one card and you apply the rule to that card. Whoever has the greatest product wins both cards. Change the rule when your child masters multiplying by the current number.

3 | Basic Facts Races

TIME: 15 minutes

MATERIALS
- markers
- paper
- index cards

Write several math problems on a piece of paper; they can be addition, subtraction, multiplication, or division—whatever your child is working on at the time. Write the answers on the index cards so that there is only one answer per card. Spread the index cards out at one end of a room.

Learning happens when: your child races to retrieve the answer to a math fact. Pick a starting point for your child, then call out a math problem. Your child should race across the room, retrieve the card with the answer, and bring it back to you. Call out a second math fact and have him race to find the answer. Continue until all the facts are used.

Variations: More competitive students may enjoy racing directly against another person, perhaps an older brother or sister.

*The physical nature of this activity appeals to students who do not like to sit still.

👁 Ask your child to help write out the problems and the answers.

👂 If your child learns by listening, have him say the fact and answer aloud.

You may want to help your child a little more if: he is having trouble finding the correct answer. Start with facts he already knows, and add only a few new facts at a time until they are all mastered.

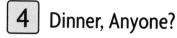

Dinner, Anyone?

Learning happens when: your child estimates the cost of dinner. Go through the sales flyer with her and make a list of the things you wish to buy from the store. Have your child estimate how much you will spend by rounding the price of each item to the nearest $0.10 or nearest $1.00, then adding the amounts.

Variations: Have your child go through a catalog to make a wish list for birthday gifts. Have her estimate how much it would cost to buy everything on the list.

✋ Ask your child to cut out pictures and prices of the items from the sales flyer. Have her divide the pictures into two groups: prices to round up and prices to round down. These steps will help clarify the task.

👁 The visual nature of the flyer should appeal to your visual learner.

👂 A catchy rhyme may help your auditory learner remember how to round. When rounding to the nearest $0.10, the last digit is the boss. When rounding to the nearest $1.00, the digit

TIME: 15–20 minutes

MATERIALS
- sales flyer from the supermarket
- paper
- pencils

to the right of the dollar amount is the boss. If the boss number is 0, 1, 2, 3, or 4, the number must be rounded down. If the boss number is 5, 6, 7, 8, or 9, the number must be rounded up. A simple rhyme about the boss is: "0, 1, 2, 3, 4, round that number down to the floor; 5, 6, 7, 8, 9, round it up and make it climb."

Mastery occurs when: your child can readily round the prices to the nearest $0.10 or $1.00, then add the amounts to estimate the total cost.

You may want to help your child a little more if: she is having trouble rounding. Practice rounding things that cost less than $1.00. Round those prices to the nearest $0.10. Once your child is comfortable with this, move on to items that cost more than $1.00. She may get confused by a price that does not need to be rounded. If the price is a nice, round number, have your child use the actual price.

 Capture Ten

TIME: 15–20 minutes

MATERIALS
▪ 10 small pieces of paper, numbered 1 through 10
▪ 3 dice
▪ paper
▪ pencils

Learning happens when: you and your child use the math operations to capture as many numbers as possible. Lay out the ten pieces of paper in numerical order. Roll the three dice. Using only the three numbers rolled, you should use addition, subtraction, multiplication, and/or division to capture as many numbers as possible. For example, if you roll the numbers 1, 2, and 3, you can capture a one $((3 - 2) \times 1 = 1)$, a two $(3 - 2 + 1 = 2)$, a three $(3 \times (2 - 1) = 3)$, a four $(3 - 1 + 2 = 4)$, a five $((3 + 2) \times 1 = 5)$, a six $(1 + 2 + 3 = 6)$, a seven $((2 \times 3) + 1 = 7)$, an eight $((3 + 1) \times$

2 = 8), a nine ((1 + 2) × 3 = 9), and a ten ((3 × 3) + 1 = 10). You get one point for each number captured. After the points are written on the paper, return the ten pieces of paper to the center of the table so that your child can use them. He plays in the same way. After five rounds, the person who captured the most numbers wins.

Variations: Work together to see how many numbers the two of you can catch. This variation appeals to students who prefer to work cooperatively.

- This game may be a little sedate, but your child will enjoy the physical aspect of rolling the dice and grabbing the numbers.
- Your visual learner may need paper on which to make his computations.
- Encourage your child to verbalize the various ways he captures a number.

Mastery occurs when: your child can use several operations to capture several numbers.

You may want to help your child a little more if: he relies on only one operation to capture a number. Work together and model how to use more than one operation to capture numbers.

6 Headline Hunt

Learning happens when: your child hunts for numbers featured in the headlines and decides whether the number is the exact amount or an estimate. For example, "Six Injured in Car

TIME: 15–20 minutes

MATERIALS
- newspapers and magazines
- rounded-edge scissors
- 2 large sheets of paper
- pencils
- nontoxic glue

Accident" would be a headline in which the reported number is an exact count. In contrast, the headline "Forest Fire Claims 3,000 Acres" is probably an estimate. The actual number of acres that burned would probably be a little more or a little less than 3,000. Your child's task is to look through old newspapers and magazines to find headlines that feature numbers and cut them out. After your child has found several headlines, she should look at each one and determine whether the number is exact or an estimate. Label one of the large pieces of paper "Exact" and the other one "Estimate." Ask your child to glue all the headlines that feature exact numbers on the "Exact" paper and all the headlines that feature estimates on the "Estimate" paper.

Variations: Ask your child to make up five headlines that feature exact numbers and five headlines that feature estimates. Mix them up and decide how you would divide the headlines into the two groups. Ask your child to check your work, then discuss any disagreement about where a headline should be.

✋ Your kinesthetic learner will enjoy this activity just the way it is. The cutting, pasting, and sorting will satisfy her need to move.

👁 Sorting the clippings into separate piles and putting them on the paper will give your child helpful visual aids.

👂 Help your child read the headlines as they are clipped. Ask her to read you the headlines that she creates. Discussion of the headlines as you sort them will also be helpful in the learning process.

Mastery occurs when: your child recognizes that sometimes numbers are reported as estimates and she can guess whether a headline contains an exact number or an estimate.

You may want to help your child a little more if: she is having difficulty determining whether a number is exact or an estimate. Go through the headlines with your child. Discuss whether the number is exact or an estimate. After the two of you have discussed all the headlines, mix them up and have her categorize them.

7 Race to Zero

Prepare the deck of cards by removing the tens and face cards. Make the aces equal to 1.

TIME: 15–20 minutes

MATERIALS
- deck of cards
- paper
- pencils

Learning happens when: you and your child play a game of subtraction. Each player gets a piece of paper and a pencil. At the top of the paper, each player should write "1,000." The object of the game is to subtract enough from 1,000 to get to zero. Shuffle the cards and place them facedown on the table. Player 1 draws two cards and makes a two-digit number from those cards. Then the player subtracts the two-digit number from 1,000. Player 2 then draws two cards, makes a two-digit number from those cards, and subtracts the number from 1,000. Player 1 then draws two cards, makes a two-digit number, and subtracts that number from the answer that resulted from the previous round. Play continues in this way until the first player subtracts enough to get to zero.

Variations: This can be turned into an addition game. Players start with zero, draw cards, create a number, then add the number until the first player gets to 1,000.

✍ Your kinesthetic learner will benefit from using the cards to create a number.

👁 Your visual learner will benefit from seeing how the cards can be changed around to create different numbers.

👂 Ask your auditory learner to verbalize the steps as he subtracts.

Mastery occurs when: your child can create the number that will best help him reach the goal of zero and can subtract the numbers without problems.

You may want to help your child a little more if: he does not create the largest number possible. Ask your child to tell you the two numbers that can be made with the cards he drew. Talk with your child about which number will help him get to zero the fastest. Also, you may want to help him a little more if he is having trouble subtracting. The biggest problem tends to be with regrouping. Help your child, step by step, until he can regroup without problems.

Number Sense and Patterns

Third graders will be required to know the place value of numbers up to the millions place. They will be asked to compare and order four-digit numbers. Third graders will also use fractions to describe sets, whole numbers, and pictures. They will begin to compare fractions and work with equivalent fractions. Your child will learn to round two-digit numbers to the nearest 10 and three-digit numbers to the nearest 100. Your child will also identify and extend whole-number patterns and geometric patterns, and she will apply a rule to input numbers in order to tell what the output should be. The table on page 103 describes some important skills related to number sense and patterns, where children can run into problems, and what you can do to help them along.

Number Sense and Pattern Skills	Having Problems?	Quick Tips
Determines the place value of numbers.	Does not understand how place value works.	Have your child color-code numbers. Write a number. Have your child trace the number using a different color marker for each place. For example, use blue for the ones place, green for the tens place, and red for the hundreds place.
Compares and orders numbers.	Cannot tell which number is largest, in the middle, and smallest.	Have your child look at the number of digits first. A three-digit number is greater than a two-digit number. If the numbers all have the same number of digits, look at the first digit of each number to determine which is higher. If the first digits are the same, move to the second digits. If the second digits are the same, move to the third digits, and so on.
Uses fractions to describe sets, whole numbers, and concrete numbers.	Does not understand how fractions work.	Working with fractions in daily life will help immensely. Bake with your child, using measuring cups. When you order a pizza, count the slices and figure out the fraction of pizza each family member will eat.
Figures out the value of a set of coins and bills.	Is confused when counting money.	Always have your child put like coins and bills together. Count the bills first, then the coins. Always start with the bill or coin that has the highest value first, moving in order down to the lowest-value bill or coin.
Identifies and extends whole-number and geometric patterns.	Is unable to see the pattern or cannot extend the pattern.	Use items such as colored candies or coins to create simple patterns. Having your child say the pattern often helps him identify it. For example, saying, "nickel, penny, nickel, penny, nickel, penny," will help your child internalize the pattern. Once your child identifies the pattern, have him say the next two items that would continue the pattern. Then add the next two items to the pattern.

(continued)

Number Sense and Pattern Skills	Having Problems?	Quick Tips
Can determine and apply rules for input and output numbers.	Is unable to look at a set of input/output numbers to determine the rule, or cannot apply the rule to a set of numbers.	Start with applying the rule. Think of a rule—for example, "add 1." Tell your child you will give her a number, and she must apply the rule and tell what the new number would be. Once your child can apply the rule, take a sheet of paper and make two columns. In column 1, write several numbers. Think of a rule, apply the rule to the numbers in column 1, and write the results in column 2. Ask your child to find the rule.

Number Sense and Patterns Activities

1 Place Value Flip

TIME: 15–20 minutes

MATERIALS
- deck of cards

Prepare the deck by removing the tens and face cards. Make the aces equal to 1.

Learning happens when: your child uses the cards to create the largest number possible. Deal all the cards equally between you and your child. Each of you will flip over three cards, create the largest number possible with those three cards, and read the number. The person who creates the largest number wins all six cards. Continue until all the cards have been played. The person who has the most cards at the end of the game wins.

Variations: You can extend this game to four-digit numbers by flipping over four cards. You can also extend this activity by awarding bonus points for adding or subtracting the two numbers created in each round.

✋ Being able to experiment with the digits by moving them around will help if your child is a mover and a shaker.

👁 Seeing how the digits can be moved around to create a number will help your visual learner.

👂 Have your auditory learner read each number aloud for additional reinforcement.

Mastery occurs when: your child knows how to arrange the cards to create the largest number possible.

You may want to help your child a little more if: he does not understand how to create the largest number. Start by flipping only two cards instead of three. Once your child is proficient at this, flip three.

2 Which Is More?

Write the following fractions on index cards: ¼, ²⁄₄, ¾, ½, ⅓, and ⅔. Turn the cards facedown on the table and mix them up.

Learning happens when: your child picks one card and measures that amount of rice and pours it into the smaller bowl. Then she picks another card and measures that amount of rice into the second bowl. Have her compare the bowls and say which bowl holds more. If the amounts are too close to judge, your child can pour them into two identical tall, slender glasses.

Variations: If you do not have rice, your child can measure dried beans, uncooked macaroni, or water.

✋ Actually measuring the rice and having a physical comparison of the fractions will help your kinesthetic learner.

TIME: 10–15 minutes

MATERIALS
- index cards
- pencils
- measuring cups
- uncooked rice in a large bowl
- two smaller bowls

👁 Seeing the amounts in the small bowls will help your visual learner get a sense of the fractions.

👂 Discuss what your child noticed while making her measurements.

Mastery occurs when: your child understands how to use the measuring cups and can successfully compare the two fractions.

You may want to help your child a little more if: she has trouble measuring. You may need to help her understand that to measure ⅔ cup, the ⅓ cup must be filled two times. Your child may also have trouble with ½ and ¼ because they are equivalent. Have her use the ¼ cup to fill the ½ cup. Measuring carefully, your child should be able to see that the two fractions are the same.

3 How Many to Make One?

Time: 10–15 minutes

MATERIALS

paper
pencils
measuring cups
uncooked rice in a large bowl

Learning happens when: your child uses various measuring cups to measure 1 cup of rice. Make a chart with two columns on your paper. Label the first column "Measuring Cup." Label the second column "How Many to Make 1 Cup." In the first column, write the following fractions: ¼, ⅓, ½. Have your child take the ¼ cup and use it to completely fill the 1-cup measuring cup. He will then write how many quarter cups it took to fill the 1-cup measuring cup. Do the same thing for the ⅓ and ½ cups.

Variations: Your child can measure other small items instead of rice.

✋ Actually measuring the rice and filling the 1-cup measuring cup will reinforce this concept with your mover and shaker.

👁 Your visual learner will benefit from seeing the relationship of the smaller measuring cups to the 1-cup measuring cup.

🎧 Try discussing your child's observations while he is measuring.

Mastery occurs when: your child understands the relationship between the denominator and how many times it took to fill 1 cup. Your child has a strong grasp of this concept if he can tell you how many times it would take to fill the 1-cup measuring cup with ⅙ cup, ⅐ cup, and so on.

You may want to help your child a little more if: he is having trouble measuring. Make sure he is filling the cups completely, with a flat top.

4 | Race to One Dollar

Learning happens when: your child exchanges smaller coins for larger coins in a race to get to one dollar. On a piece of paper, make a chart that looks like this:

Pennies	Nickels	Dimes	Quarters	$1.00

TIME: 15–20 minutes

MATERIALS
- 6 pennies
- 3 nickels
- 3 dimes
- 4 quarters
- dollar bill
- paper
- pencils
- 1 die

Have your child roll the die. Give her the same number of cents as the number that was rolled—for example, roll a 3, get three cents. Have your child put the coins on the chart. Roll again, adding cents to the chart. After each roll, your child should make all exchanges possible—for example, if she has five pennies, those pennies must be exchanged for a nickel, two nickels must be exchanged for a dime, and so on. After exchanges are made, have your child count the money on the chart. Play continues until the coins on the chart add up to one dollar.

✋ Your mover and shaker will particularly enjoy working with real money.

👁 Your visual learner will like the organization the chart provides.

👂 Ask your child to count the money aloud.

Mastery occurs when: your child understands how to make exchanges and can easily count the money on the chart.

You may want to help your child a little more if: she is having trouble with the exchanges or with the counting. Play the game only exchanging coins. If exchanging coins is a problem, trace a penny five times in the pennies column of the chart. Trace a nickel two times in the nickels column. Trace a dime two times in the dimes column. Trace a quarter four times in the quarters column.

Pennies	Nickels	Dimes	Quarters	$1.00

Ask your child to place the coins in a circle. When the circles are full in any one part, it's time to exchange. The only exception is that two dimes and one nickel must be exchanged for a quarter. If your child is having trouble counting the money, count it with her, always starting from the right side of the chart and moving left.

5 | What's My Rule?

Learning happens when: your child gives you numbers and can use the output numbers to determine what rule you are applying. Tell your child it's time for "What's My Rule?" You think of a rule, such as "add three." Your child gives you a number. You apply the rule mentally and give your child the output number. For example, your child says, "1." You mentally add three and tell your child, "4." Your child then gives you another number, you apply the rule, and give the output number. This continues until your child believes he knows the rule. At that point, you give him a number. Your child mentally applies the rule he believes is correct and gives you the output number. If he is right, ask him to tell you the rule in words. If your child is incorrect, play continues. This activity will be difficult at first, but it gets easier with practice.

Variations: Once your child understands how the game works, ask him to think of a rule, and play so that you are trying to determine the rule.

TIME: 5 minutes

- Kinesthetic learners will enjoy using manipulatives (things that he can hold and count) to represent the input and output numbers.

- Your visual learner may need to write down the input and output numbers to determine the rule. This is fine, but try to encourage him to do it mentally once he is comfortable doing it on paper.

- Ask your child to verbalize the input number and the output number. For example, have your child say, "A three goes in and a five comes out."

Mastery occurs when: your child can figure out a rule after three or four numbers.

You may want to help your child a little more if: he is having trouble determining the rule. Start with very simple rules. If your child still has trouble, try doing only addition rules. Then move on to the other operations as your child gets more comfortable.

6 Input/Output Machine

TIME: 45–60 minutes

MATERIALS
- quart-size milk carton
- knife
- tape
- strip of heavy paper that is the width of the milk carton and 6 inches long
- strip of heavy paper that is the width of the milk carton and 4 inches long
- index cards
- rounded-edge scissors
- markers

Thoroughly clean the milk carton and let it dry. With a knife, carefully cut a rectangular slot in the milk carton. The slot should be about 3 or 4 inches wide, ¼ inch tall, and located about one-third of the way from the top of the milk carton. Cut a second slot that is the same size located about two-thirds of the way from the top of the milk carton. It will look something like this:

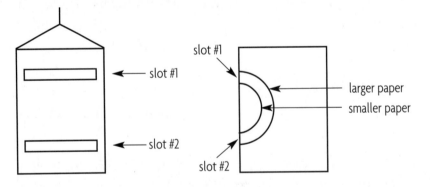

Open the top of the milk carton. You are now going to make a chute that will connect slot #1 to slot #2. Tape the bottom of the larger strip of paper to the bottom of slot #2. Tape the bottom of the smaller strip of paper to the top of slot #2. Now, take the top of the smaller strip of paper, and tape it to the bottom of slot #1. Finally, take the top of the larger strip of paper, and tape it to the top of slot #1. The strips of paper should form a chute, through which the index cards will travel. You may need to adjust the length of the strips of paper so that the chute is the correct size and the index card can travel through it without getting caught. Cut the index cards in half. Think of several simple rules to apply to numbers such as +1, +5, +10, −2, −3, ×2, and so on. Take five to seven half-size index cards. Put a dot on one side in the upper right-hand corner. The dot will show your child which side is the top of the card. Put a different number on the top side of each card. Flip the cards over. On the bottoms of the cards, put the results of applying one of the rules to the number on top. You'll need to make a set of cards for each rule. One card set may look something like this:

Rule: Multiply the input number by 2.

Tops of the Cards:

| 1 | 3 | 5 | 7 | 9 | 11 | 13 |

Bottoms of the Cards:

| 2 | 6 | 10 | 14 | 18 | 22 | 26 |

Make several sets of cards. Use a different color marker for each rule so that if the cards get mixed up, they can easily be put back into sets according to color. Make an answer key for yourself. Note the color and the rule on your answer key. This will help you keep everything straight.

Learning happens when: your child uses the input/output milk carton machine to determine a rule for a set of numbers. Have her organize the cards so that all the dots are facing up. Have her say the number on top and put the card in the top slot. The card will travel down the chute, turn over, and come out of the bottom slot with the bottom of the card now facing up. Have your child say the output number. Your child may say, "In goes a one [she should now put the card in the top slot] and out comes a two." Continue with the other numbers. After all the cards for that set have gone through the chute, have your child tell you what rule the input/output machine has applied.

Variations: This activity can be modified to be very simple or very complicated, depending on the needs of your child. She can create sets of cards for the machine. Let your child see if you can figure out the rule. You can truly gauge your child's understanding by having her create the cards.

- Your kinesthetic learner will love the physical aspect of the machine flipping the cards over.

- Ask your child to decorate the box. Seeing the numbers change as the card travels through the machine will help your child "see" the rule better.

- Ask your child to verbalize what is happening to the card. This will help her sort out what is happening.

Mastery occurs when: your child can figure out the rule of each of the sets of cards.

You may want to help your child a little more if: she is having trouble figuring out the rule. Ask your child if the numbers are getting larger or smaller. If the numbers are getting larger, that's a clue that either addition or multiplication is involved. If the numbers are getting smaller, that's a clue that either subtraction or division is involved. Once the rule is narrowed down to two operations, have your child keep track of the input/output numbers on paper. Seeing all of them at once may help her figure out the relationship.

7   How Many Ways?

Learning happens when: your child uses the coins to find several ways to make a certain amount of money. Have him write the title "Ways to Make _____" on a sheet of paper. Make four columns under the title. Label them "Quarters," "Dimes," "Nickels," and "Pennies." The page will look something like this:

Time: 15–20 minutes

Materials
- several coins of differing values
- small pad of paper
- store flyer

Ways to Make _____

Quarters	Dimes	Nickles	Pennies

Have your child look through the store flyer for an item that costs less than a dollar. Write the price of the item in the title at the top of the paper. Have your child use the coins to figure out at least three ways to make that amount of money. Note how many quarters, dimes, nickels, and pennies are needed for each way. The final sheet of paper may look like this:

Ways to Make $0.99

Quarters	Dimes	Nickels	Pennies
3	2	0	4
3	1	2	4
2	4	1	4

Start a new sheet and pick a different item from the flyer, then follow the same process to find different ways to combine coins to make that amount.

Variations: This activity can easily be modified to use bills instead of coins.

✋ Having the coins available for this activity will help your kinesthetic learner.

👁 Keeping the information organized in table form may help your visual learner see patterns in counting money, such as one dime can be replaced with two nickels, one nickel and five pennies, or ten pennies.

👂 Ask your child to count the money aloud to help find the correct number of coins.

Mastery occurs when: your child can find several ways to make a certain amount of money.

You may want to help your child a little more if: he is having trouble finding several ways to make a certain amount of money. Work with your child, helping him count out the money. You may also want to limit the coins to nickels and pennies at first. Once your child is comfortable finding an amount using only nickels and pennies, add dimes. After he has used dimes, nickels, and pennies, add quarters.

Geometry and Measurement

In second grade, your child learned to name, describe, and compare shapes, and learned about the concept of passing time using a clock and a calendar. She learned how to find the perimeter of simple shapes and how to read a thermometer. This year your child will be asked to name, describe, and compare both shapes and solids; figure elapsed time; measure to the nearest half inch; and find both perimeter and area. She will also be asked to identify congruent figures, find lines of symmetry, and read a coordinate graph. The following table describes some important skills related to geometry and measurement, where children can run into problems, and what you can do to help them along.

Geometry and Measurement Skills	Having Problems?	Quick Tips
Names, describes, and compares shapes and solids.	Has trouble telling the difference between a shape and a solid.	Help your child understand that a shape is flat and a solid is three-dimensional. Draw different shapes, such as a square, a rectangle, a circle, a triangle, a rhombus, and a parallel-ogram, on a piece of paper. Gather examples of a cube, a rectangular prism, a cone, a cylinder, a sphere, and a pyramid. Show your child how solids can be held, but shapes are flat.
Identifies congruent shapes.	Has trouble understanding the concept of congruence.	To reinforce that congruent means same size and same shape, draw several pairs of congruent figures. Have your child cut out the figures and lay one on top of the other to prove the figures are congruent.
Determines lines of symmetry.	Has trouble determining if a shape has a line of symmetry.	Have your child fold a piece of paper in half. Cut out various shapes along the fold such as hearts, snowflakes, and so on. Open the shape, and the fold line is the line of symmetry. Look for other items that have a line of symmetry.

(continued)

Geometry and Measurement Skills	Having Problems?	Quick Tips
Measures to the nearest half inch, foot, yard, centimeter, decimeter, and meter.	Has trouble measuring.	Make sure your child is holding the ruler correctly. Also, make sure the starting point of the ruler is lined up with the edge of the item being measured. This concept is best learned through direct experience, so have your child measure as many things as possible in daily life.
Finds the perimeter and area of rectangles.	Confuses perimeter and area.	Perimeter has the word "rim" in it. Explain to your child that he should think of a basketball rim. The rim is the outside part only. Perimeter is measuring only the "rim" of a shape. For area, your child could think of an area rug. An area rug covers the floor, so area is the measurement of how much it takes to completely cover a shape.
Uses a thermometer to measure temperature.	Has trouble reading a thermometer.	It can be confusing to read a thermometer, because most of the marks are not numbered. Get a thermometer and help your child make sense of all the marks. Have her read the air temperature daily.
Finds the points on a coordinate graph.	Confuses the numbers of the ordered pair.	Get a simple map that has coordinates along the bottom and the side. Find the coordinates for different places on the map. When giving the two coordinates, make sure your child gives the coordinate from the bottom first, then the coordinate from the side.

Geometry and Measurement Activities

1 Hunt for Solids

Write the following six solids on the index cards: cube, rectangular prism, cone, cylinder, sphere, and pyramid. Draw a picture of some examples of the solids on the back of each index card.

TIME: 10–15 minutes

MATERIALS
6 index cards

Learning happens when: your child hunts the house for samples of the solids he will be learning about this year. Help him understand the following: a cube has square faces like a die; a rectangular prism is shaped like a box; a cone looks like an ice-cream cone or a party hat; a cylinder is in the shape of a drum or a toilet paper tube; a sphere is shaped like a ball; and a pyramid has a square base with triangular sides that come up to a point. Give your child the index cards and have him search the house for at least two examples of each of the solids.

Variations: If your child loves to race the clock, set the kitchen timer for five or ten minutes.

- Your child will enjoy the hunt and feeling the solids.
- Ask your visual learner to help you make the index cards.
- Ask your child to tell you which items go with which shape and why.

Mastery occurs when: your child can find at least two examples of each solid.

You may want to help your child a little more if: he is having trouble finding items that fit. Examples of a pyramid may be difficult to find, but your home is full of examples of the other solids. Do the search with your child. Find one or two things together, and ask him to find a third on his own.

2 Solid Concentration

TIME: 10–15 minutes

MATERIALS
- 12 index cards
- pencils
- magazines
- nontoxic glue

On six of the cards, write the following solids: cube, rectangular prism, cone, cylinder, sphere, and pyramid. On the other six cards, draw or glue a picture of the following: an item that is a cube, an item that is a rectangular prism, an item that is a cone, an item that is a cylinder, an item that is a sphere, and an item that is a pyramid. Be careful that the pictures are of three-dimensional solid objects, not simple shapes.

Learning happens when: your child matches the name of the solid with its picture in the classic game of concentration. Shuffle the cards and place them facedown in a 3 × 4 grid—that is, individually laid out in three columns and four rows. Player 1 turns over two cards. If the name matches the picture, the player keeps both cards. If there is no match, the cards are turned back over, and player 2 takes a turn. Continue playing until all matches have been made. The person who collects the most cards wins.

Variations: Ask your child to go through old magazines and cut out pictures of the solids to glue onto the six picture cards.

- Your mover and shaker will enjoy games that require her to physically do something. The act of flipping over the cards and remembering the placement of the cards will benefit your child.

- Your visual learner will receive reinforcement by linking the shape word with a picture of the shape.

- Ask your child to tell you why a picture does or does not match the shape word.

Mastery occurs when: your child can quickly tell whether the picture card matches the word card.

You may want to help your child a little more if: she is having difficulty making the matches. Play the game faceup until your child can match the picture to the name quickly. When your child feels she can match the cards fairly easily, begin playing the traditional method.

3 | What Time Will It End?

On several index cards, write different activities and different times. For example, on one card write, "Brush your teeth—5 minutes." On another card write, "Soccer practice—1 hour." On a third card write, "Eat lunch—25 minutes." Continue until you have several activities and times.

TIME: 10–15 minutes

MATERIALS
index cards
paper
pencils

Learning happens when: your child can determine an ending time when given the starting time of an activity and how long the activity lasts. Shuffle the index cards and place them facedown. Write a starting time at the top of the paper. Player 1 draws a card, reads the activity and time, and figures out the ending time. He then writes the ending time on the paper. Player 2 draws a card and figures the ending time based on the time last written by player 1. Player 2 writes the new ending time on the paper. Play continues until all the cards have been used.

Variation: Try this activity with just one player. Your child can calculate the ending times on his own.

 Your active learner may like to use a toy clock to help him figure the ending times.

👁 Your visual learner may need a more organized paper on which to write the starting and ending times. Create a three-column table in which the first column is "Starting Time," the second column is "Length of Activity," and the third column is "Ending Time." Use the table to keep track of the work.

🎧 Encourage your child to talk aloud as he is computing the ending times.

Mastery occurs when: your child can readily figure each ending time.

You may want to help your child a little more if: he is having trouble figuring out ending times. Start with times that are easier to compute, such as only whole hours or half-hours. Once your child is comfortable with this, add cards with times that are not so tidy.

4 | Let's Decorate the Perimeter!

Time: 15–20 minutes

MATERIALS
- rounded-edge scissors
- construction paper
- ruler
- ribbon
- nontoxic glue

Cut the construction paper into several different sizes of rectangles and squares. Make sure the sides of the shapes measure to the whole inch. For example, cut one square with sides of 4 inches, a rectangle that is 4 inches by 6 inches, and so on.

Learning happens when: your child decorates the inside perimeter of the shapes. Have her measure the sides of one of the construction paper shapes. Then have her add the measurements for each side together to calculate the perimeter. She should then measure and cut the ribbon to go around the inside perimeter and glue it down.

Variation: You can use almost anything to decorate the perimeter, such as rickrack, fringe, and so on.

✋ This activity is great for your kinesthetic learner. By measuring and decorating the perimeter, your child will get real hands-on experience of what the perimeter is and how to find it.

👁 Your visual child will love doing this project and having these decorated papers to use for writing notes or as a frame for pictures.

👂 Ask your child to verbalize the steps as she completes them.

Mastery occurs when: your child can successfully measure the perimeter, then measure and cut the ribbon to match the perimeter.

You may want to help your child a little more if: she is over-whelmed. Have your child measure the perimeter and tell you how many inches of ribbon to cut. Cut exactly the number of inches she asked you to cut. It will be readily apparent if she did not measure the perimeter accurately.

5 | What's the Temperature?

Prepare the graph paper by writing a title, such as "Daily Temperature." Along the bottom, write the dates for one week from left to right. Along the side, write a temperature scale.

TIME: 10 minutes each day

MATERIALS
- graph paper
- pencils
- outdoor thermometer
- ruler

Learning happens when: your child reads the air temperature daily and graphs the results. At the same time each day, have him read the temperature on an outdoor thermometer. Then have him put a large dot on the intersection of that day's date and temperature. The next day, do the same thing, and have him use a ruler to connect yesterday's dot to today's dot. Continue daily, and your child will have created a line graph. If this is done for a long period of time, your child will be able to see patterns in the temperature according to the time of year.

Variations: Instead of a line graph, your child can keep a two-column table in which the first column is the date and the second column is the temperature.

✋ Making this a task to complete every day will help your kinesthetic learner.

👁 Your visual learner will have a real sense of accomplishment as he sees the graph grow larger.

👂 Encourage your child to read the date and temperature aloud.

Mastery occurs when: your child can read the thermometer and record the temperature on the graph accurately.

You may want to help your child a little more if: he is having difficulty either reading the thermometer or recording the temperature on the graph. Complete this task with your child for several days until he is ready to do it alone.

6 | Symmetry Hunt

TIME: 20–30 minutes

MATERIALS
- 2 large sheets of paper or poster board
- markers
- magazines
- rounded-edge scissors
- nontoxic glue

Write the title "Symmetrical" on the top of one of the large sheets of paper. Write "Not Symmetrical" on the top of the other sheet of paper. Lay the sheets of paper down on the floor or a table.

Learning happens when: your child hunts through old magazines to find pictures of items that have symmetry and items that do not have symmetry. As your child finds pictures, she should cut them out and place them on the correct paper (do not glue yet). After several pictures have been placed on each of the pieces of paper, have your child go through each of the symmetrical pictures and explain to you where the lines of symmetry are located. Have her show you the pictures that do not have symmetry. After you and your child have discussed each of the pictures and have determined that they are on the correct posters, have her glue the pictures down. Now your child has two posters to remind her about symmetry.

Variations: If this activity is too easy for your child, ask her to divide the symmetrical pictures according to the number of lines of symmetry using several posters, with titles such as "Not Symmetrical," "One Line of Symmetry," "Two Lines of Symmetry," "Three Lines of Symmetry," and so on.

- Your child will enjoy and learn from hunting for and cutting out items for the posters.

- Your visual learner will like working with the pictures and will probably be able to see the lines of symmetry better than kinesthetic or auditory learners.

- Encourage your auditory child to think aloud as she is hunting for the pictures.

Mastery occurs when: your child can look at a picture and tell whether the item has symmetry or does not have symmetry.

You may want to help your child a little more if: she is having trouble determining if an item has a line of symmetry. Give her a small mirror. Have her hold the mirror upright on the imaginary line that goes down the middle of the image. Have her look at the mirror and compare it to the other side of the figure. If the mirror is on the line of symmetry, the image in the mirror will look just like the other side of the figure. A line of symmetry can be vertical, horizontal, or diagonal. Your child may need to test several lines to see if there is a line of symmetry.

7 | What's My Area?

Learning happens when: your child uses the tiles to find the area of various items. The area is found by seeing how many squares it takes to cover a figure. Have your child find the area of an index

TIME: 10–15 minutes

MATERIALS

■ several tiles that are 1-inch squares (available at home improvement or education supply stores, or you can cut out your own from newspaper by using the pattern at www.knowledge essentials.com)

■ various small, flat items to measure, such as an index card or a book

card, a photograph, the cover of a book, the top of a jewelry box, and so on. Remind your child that he must use the squares to cover the whole item, with no gaps between the squares. This activity works best if the items are either square or rectangular, and the items' dimensions are to the nearest whole inch.

Variations: Use 1-foot squares (cut from newspaper) to find the area of larger things such as an area rug, a room, and so on.

🖐 Using the physical squares will help your kinesthetic learner understand how area is measured.

👁 Seeing the grid formed by the square will help your child see how area works.

🖐 Ask your child to explain how area is measured to help him understand it.

Mastery occurs when: your child can use the squares to measure area and doesn't confuse area with perimeter. True mastery occurs when your child can tell you that perimeter is only concerned with the outer edges of a figure, while area is concerned with covering a figure completely.

You may want to help your child a little more if: he is having trouble understanding area. Work with your child to find the area of one or two things, then ask him to find the area of a third thing.

Probability and Statistics

You are probably thinking, probability and statistics? No way! But it is a part of third grade math. Your child will start with the concepts of always, sometimes, and never. For example, he should be able to tell you that "My dog began speaking French last night" will never happen; "It rains on Tuesdays" sometimes happens; and "Summer break comes

Probability and Statistics Skills	Having Problems?	Quick Tips
Collects, organizes, and records data.	Is overwhelmed and does not know what to do first.	Have your child collect data about daily life. For example, have your child record how many commercials are shown during her favorite TV show. Do this for several shows, and make a table showing the names of the shows and how many commercials aired during each.
Reads and interprets tables, graphs, and charts.	Is confused by what tables are showing.	At every opportunity, read tables with your child. There are plenty out there: practice schedules, lunch menus, sports statistics, and so on.
Describes events as more likely, less likely, or equally likely.	Is confused by the language.	Use these terms frequently so that your child hears them. For example, "The forecast says it is more likely to be sunny tomorrow than rainy"; "I am less likely to let you play if your room is not clean."
Computes permutations of up to three items.	Misses some of the items.	Pull out something your child can manipulate with his hands. For example, give your child three different color beads and ask him to find how many different ways there are to put the beads on a necklace. (There are always six ways with three items.)

after the school year ends" always happens. Once children understand the concepts of always, sometimes, and never, they move on to the concepts of more likely, less likely, and equally likely. Your child will be asked questions such as, "Is it more likely to snow during the summer or the winter?" The questions will become more complex, until your child will be asked to look at a spinner and tell which color is more or less likely to be spun. He will be collecting, organizing, and recording data. Data aren't scary; they are just the answers to questions. Finally, your child will learn about permutations, a total number of groupings into which a group of elements can be arranged, of up to three items. For example, how many numbers can be created with the digits 3, 4, and 5? Six numbers can be created—345, 354, 435, 453, 534, and 543. The table on page 125 describes some important skills related to probability and statistics, where children can run into problems, and what you can do to help them along.

Probability and Statistics Activities

1 Stop and Go Traffic

TIME: Varies

MATERIALS
- paper
- pencils

Draw three columns on the paper. Label one column "Red," one column "Yellow," and one column "Green."

Learning happens when: your child keeps track of the number of red, yellow, and green lights encountered during a car trip. As you approach an intersection, have him put a tally mark under the correct color. To extend the activity, your child can then create a bar graph that shows how many lights were red, how many were yellow, and how many were green.

Variations: Ask your child to keep track of how many lights you encounter on trips you make frequently. For example, how many lights do you pass going to school? How many lights are passed going to the grocery store? How many lights are passed going to Aunt Mary's house? Then your child can create a table that shows the destination and how many lights are between your house and the destination.

This task will give your kinesthetic learner something to do and will keep him busy in the car.

👁 Your visual learner will enjoy seeing the data organized in the table and the bar graph.

👂 Give your child reminders to write down the data as you approach the lights and have him tell you at the end of the trip how many lights were each color.

Mastery occurs when: your child can collect and organize the information and put it in a form that is easy to understand.

You may want to help your child a little more if: he is having trouble completing the task. When approaching an intersection, ask your child in which column the tally mark will go. When the trip is over, he may need help creating a bar graph. You can use a spreadsheet program on a computer, or there is a great Web site that will allow him to create many different kinds of graphs, www. nces.ed.gov/nceskids/graphing.

2 | My Poll

Learning happens when: your child develops and conducts a survey and graphs the results. Have her think of a topic about which she wants to get other people's opinions. It can be very simple, such as finding out people's favorite season, sport, color, movie, and so on. Your child can ask what would be someone's dream job or dream vacation, or if people prefer cats or dogs. Once she decides on a question, have her ask several friends or family members. She should keep track of the answers. After everyone has been polled, have your child create a table and/or graph to show the information.

Variations: A child who is very shy probably will not enjoy doing this type of activity. Instead, she could find examples of tables and

TIME: 15–20 minutes

MATERIALS
- paper
- pencils
- graph paper

graphs that give information about people's opinions in the newspaper or a magazine. Ask your child to search for a graph, read it, and tell you what the graph shows.

- ✍ Your kinesthetic learner will enjoy using a pretend or real microphone to interview or poll the people for her survey.

- 👁 Organizing the results in table or list form will help your visual learner.

- 👂 Your auditory child will love asking people for their opinions. Let her record the answers and play them back.

Mastery occurs when: your child can develop questions for a survey, conduct the poll, and put the information in a table or graph that is easy to understand.

You may want to help your child a little more if: she is having trouble completing this task. Make sure your child understands that there are three different tasks: (1) thinking of a question, (2) gathering the information, and (3) showing the information. Organization is the key. Help her by explaining step by step how to do this activity in a very organized way.

 **3** Coin Flip

TIME: 15–20 minutes

MATERIALS
- coin
- paper
- pencils

Learning happens when: your child performs an experiment to see how many times heads is flipped and how many times tails is flipped. Have him prepare for the experiment by writing two columns on the paper. Label the first column "Heads" and the second column "Tails." As the coin is flipped, tally the number of heads and the number of tails. After ten trials, how many are heads and how many are tails? Do the numbers match what you thought would happen? After your child has answered those two questions, continue flipping the coin until you have completed fifty trials. Again, how many are heads and how many are tails? Do the numbers match what you thought would happen? Then continue flipping until you have completed a hundred trials. How many are heads and how many are tails? Explain to your child that the probability is that the coin will land on heads half the time and tails half the time. The results probably did not match the probability after ten trials, but they should have been fairly close after a hundred trials.

Variations: Spin the coin a hundred times and see how many times it lands on heads and how many times it lands on tails. You would expect heads half the time and tails half the time. It does not work out this way with spinning the coin because there isn't an equal amount of weight on each side of the coin. Tails (the lighter side) should show up more than heads. Do your child's results show this?

- Your kinesthetic learner will love flipping a coin.
- Encourage your child to organize results neatly on the paper.
- Ask your child to discuss his results with you.

Mastery occurs when: your child can keep track of the data and can compare his data with the probability.

You may want to help your child a little more if: it is too difficult or time-consuming to flip and tally a hundred times. Have him flip the coin ten or twenty times while you keep track of the results. Then switch roles so that you flip the coin ten or twenty times, and have your child keep track of the results.

How Likely?

TIME: 15–20 minutes

MATERIALS
- 2 paper plates
- pencils
- index cards

On one paper plate, write "Likely." On the other paper plate, write "Unlikely." On the index cards write several events, such as, "It will snow tomorrow"; "I will go to school tomorrow"; "Mom will buy a new car today"; "I will fly in a plane next week"; "I will brush my teeth tonight"; "I will wear a coat today."

Learning happens when: your child categorizes events as likely or unlikely. Have her mix up the index cards, pick one, and put it on the appropriate paper plate depending on whether the event is likely or unlikely to happen. After your child has categorized each event, ask her to explain why she chose to categorize it in that way.

Variations: Ask your child to write down some events for you to categorize as likely or unlikely.

Moving the events to the proper plate helps keep your kinesthetic learner enthusiastic about this activity.

Try using a chart to let your child record answers in a way that is easy to view them.

Discussing the reasons for the choices will help your auditory learner understand the difference between likely and unlikely.

Mastery occurs when: your child can categorize an event as likely or unlikely and give supporting reasons for her choices.

You may want to help your child a little more if: she is having trouble categorizing the events. As simple as it seems, this concept can be surprisingly difficult for a child. Check to make sure she understands the terms "likely" and "unlikely." Explain that "likely" means probably yes. "Unlikely" means probably no. If your child understands the words but is still having trouble, go through a few of the event cards with her. If the event is something like "I will go to school tomorrow," ask your child, "Do you think you will go to school tomorrow?" The answer could be yes or no. Ask your child to explain her answer. If the explanation is reasonable, accept it. Have your child put the event on the appropriate plate.

5 What's in the Bag?

TIME: 10–15 minutes

MATERIALS
- 10 marbles in two different colors (more of one than the other)
- sack or paper bag
- paper
- pencils

Put the marbles in the bag. Make sure there is clearly more of one color marble—for example, you may put seven green marbles and three orange marbles in the bag. Your child should not see you put the marbles in the bag.

Learning happens when: your child uses probability to figure out what is in the bag. Have him draw a marble from the bag without looking, write the color on the paper, and make a tally mark for that color. Put the marble back in the bag, shake, and have your child draw another marble. If it is the same color, have him make another tally mark for that color. If it is a different color, have him write the new color on the paper and make a tally mark for that color. Put the marble back in the bag, shake, and have your child draw another marble. Continue in this fashion until he has blindly drawn a marble twenty times. Tell your child there are ten marbles in the bag. Have him use the results to predict how many of each color are in the bag.

Variations: You can use other items besides marbles. Just make sure they are uniform in size and shape so that your child cannot tell the difference of the items by touch.

✍ Your child will understand probability better by doing this activity rather than just reading or hearing about probability.

👁 Keeping track of the results with tallies will help your visual learner predict the colors in the bag.

👂 Ask your child to talk through his results.

Mastery occurs when: your child can make a reasonable prediction based on his results.

You may want to help your child a little more if: he is having trouble predicting. Instead of predicting the number of marbles for each color, have him predict the color of most marbles. After your child can successfully predict which color there is more of, have him start predicting how many there are of that color.

6 | Clothes Horse

TIME: 10–15 minutes

MATERIALS
▫ 2 different hats
▫ 3 different jackets
▫ paper
▫ pencils

Learning happens when: your child tries on the clothing items to figure out how many different combinations of hats and jackets she can wear. Lay out the clothes. Tell your child to figure out how many different looks she can create with the clothing items. She should figure out that with one of the hats, there are three different looks (hat #1/jacket #1; hat #1/jacket #2; hat #1/jacket #3). There are three additional looks with hat #2 (hat #2/jacket #1; hat #2/jacket #2; hat #2/jacket #3). So there are a total of six different looks, or permutations.

Variations: You could use the same concept with other items of clothing, such as shorts and shirts or shoes and socks. Add to the total number of items.

✋ Movers and shakers will really enjoy this activity. Actually trying on the clothes will help your child understand this concept.

👁 Ask your child to try drawing a picture of the combinations or laying each outfit on the bed to see how many different combinations there are.

👂 Encourage your child to verbalize the combinations (red hat, blue jacket; red hat, green jacket; red hat, black jacket; orange hat, blue jacket; orange hat, green jacket; orange hat, black jacket).

Mastery occurs when: your child can figure out all of the possible permutations.

You may want to help your child a little more if: she cannot figure out the total number of combinations. Help her perform this task in a more organized way. It is much easier to find all the combinations with one item (the hat) first before changing to the second item (the other hat.)

7 | Snack Attack

Learning happens when: your child determines how many different combinations of snacks can be made with three types of fruits and two types of drinks. Have him put one fruit on the plate and one drink on the coaster. That represents one snack your child could have. Then have him keep the same fruit on the plate but change the drink. That is a second snack your child could have. Have your child continue until he finds all the different combinations of snacks. (There are six. To find how many different combinations, figure out how many different items are in each category and multiply the numbers together. Three fruits times two drinks equals six combinations.) After all the combinations have been found, let your child pick his favorite to have as a snack.

TIME: 10–15 minutes

MATERIALS

▪ 3 types of fruit
▪ 2 types of drinks
▪ plate
▪ drink coaster
▪ paper
▪ pencils

Variations: This activity can be done with any kinds of food. Your child can find the combinations of lunches served in the cafeteria.

For example, if a cafeteria has two entrees to choose from (hamburger or pizza), two vegetables to choose from (french fries or corn), and two drinks to choose from (milk or water), there are eight different combinations. (Two entrees times two vegetables times two drinks equals eight combinations.)

✋ Actually moving the fruit to the plate and the drink to the coaster will help your kinesthetic child understand how permutations work.

👁 Your visual child may want to write down the combinations as he creates them in order to keep track of how many permutations there are.

👂 Your auditory child may need to think aloud and say the combinations.

Mastery occurs when: your child understands what permutations are and can successfully find all the combinations.

You may want to help your child a little more if: he is having trouble finding the combinations. Encourage your child to be organized. Do not let him change the fruit until he finds all the combinations for it.

Environmental Learning

Daily life provides so many opportunities to talk about math. A perfect example is while you're driving in the car. You could discuss the probability of hitting a red light, the time it takes to get somewhere, how much gas you will use, how much the gas costs, and so on. When you stop at a store, you could discuss what you will buy, how much it will cost, and how to calculate the tax. Think about all of the math concepts you use without thinking about them all day long, then start talking about them with your child.

End of Third Grade Math Checklist

Students who are working at the standard level at the end of third grade:

_____ Comfortably add and subtract large numbers

_____ Know the basic multiplication and division facts

_____ Understand how place value works in our number system

_____ Round numbers in order to make a reasonable estimate

_____ Use tools such as rulers and thermometers to measure the area and perimeter of squares and rectangles

_____ Differentiate solids from shapes

_____ Find fractions of a whole and fractions of a set

_____ Understand basic probability and statistics

_____ Understand how bar graphs, line graphs, and tables communicate information in math

Third Grade Science 8

Your third grader will have a new emphasis on science this year. During second grade, science often alternates with social studies. In third grade, science has a bigger part of the week. Your child will extend science concepts introduced in second grade, as well as learn many new concepts and experiences. Third grade science can be divided into two broad categories: science processes and science concepts. Some science processes include evidence, models, measurement, form and function, and explanation. Science concepts your child will learn this year include simple systems and subsystems; how sound is produced and how it travels; the characteristics, basic needs, and habitats of organisms; and forces that change the earth, such as earthquakes and glaciers.

Science Processes

One of the most important things for your budding scientist to do is observe. This can be a harder skill than you think, particularly for aural

Science Processes Skills	Having Problems?	Quick Tips
Observes.	Does not often notice things.	Ask your child about changes around him. These can be changes in the house, out in the yard, and so on. Play games that rely on observation, such as "I Spy."
Measures.	Does not know what tool to use to measure; does not know the units of measurement.	Measurement is a skill best developed by real-world practice. Have your child help measure things around the house. She can help measure a wall to see if a piece of furniture would fit, measure items for cooking, and so on.
Classifies.	Has trouble classifying items.	Every house has a junk drawer. Open the junk drawer, and have your child organize it, putting like items together. Your child could also organize his closet, putting summer clothes together and winter clothes together, or even sort laundry. Look for opportunities for your child to organize by classifying items.
Conducts an experiment.	Has trouble following the scientific method.	Make sure your child conducts an experiment step by step. Have her show you that each step is complete before being allowed to move to the next step.

and kinesthetic learners. Kids are naturally curious, but sometimes they need help in examining things in detail. Third grade science is where we really start trying to harness and refine some skills that your child comes by naturally. You can help by encouraging her to notice things and to find out why things happen.

The first step of the scientific method is observation. Helping your child classify what she observes is part of the process. It helps her relate the new observations to previous knowledge and/or new ideas. Measuring becomes more important in third grade science, refining and extending skills that your child has been working on since kindergarten. Your child will learn to measure length in meters or centimeters, mass in grams, and temperature in degrees Celsius. Being able to read different types of charts, graphs, and tables is a skill that is necessary in all subjects: math, reading, social studies, and science.

This year your child will begin conducting simple experiments. While she will not be required to follow the scientific method precisely, she will need to be able to plan and conduct a simple investigation, then communicate the results. The natural curiosity of children provides many opportunities to conduct a simple investigation. "I wonder what will happen if . . ." is a great way to start a science experiment at home or at school. The table on page 138 describes some important skills related to science processes, where children can run into problems, and what you can do to help them along.

Science Processes Activities

1 Nature Detective

Learning happens when: your child keeps a journal that details the observations he makes about nature over a period of time. This is a great activity for the fall or spring, when there is a lot of activity in nature. Have your child pick something he will watch and write about for a period of time. Choices can include observing a bird's nest, watching the activities of a squirrel, keeping track of the organisms that are living under a rock, or noting how the tomato plant is growing in the garden. There is no limit to what your child can observe. Have him spend five or ten minutes for two or three days a week observing, then writing about and

TIME: Varies

MATERIALS
- notebook
- pencils

drawing a picture of his observations. Finally, ask your child to tell you about what he has noticed.

✋ Kinesthetic learners may find it difficult to sit quietly and observe, but getting them outside to observe something may help.

👁 Your child will excel at visual observations and will enjoy having a nice journal in which to record observations. Let him decorate the journal or purchase one that he likes.

👂 Your auditory learner may enjoy recording observations on a tape recorder.

Mastery occurs when: your child can observe and communicate his observations.

You may want to help your child a little more if: he does not know what to write or talk about. Observe with your child. Have him notice and record the smallest changes. Model being observant by stating things you notice. Once your child hones his observation skills, he will notice all kinds of things.

2 | Germination Bags

TIME: A few minutes
each day

MATERIALS
▢ paper towel
▢ plastic zip-top sand-
wich bag
▢ 2 or 3 seeds (such as
bean seeds)
▢ notebook
▢ pencils

Learning occurs when: your child germinates (starts developing) seeds in a plastic bag and keeps notes of her daily observations. Have her moisten the paper towel. Make sure it is damp but not sopping wet. If the towel is too wet, the seeds may rot. Fold the paper towel into fourths and place it in the plastic bag. Take two or three seeds and place them in the plastic bag. Put the bag in a safe place that receives sunlight. Have your child write down in her notebook how the germination bag was made. Every day at about the same time, have her write the date and record any changes she notices.

Variations: Use a seed that quickly grows very tall, such as beans or peas. To quicken germination, soak the bean seeds in water for several hours. Then plant them in a paper cup filled three-quarters of the way with potting soil. Plant the seeds about one inch deep. Ask your child to measure how many millimeters the plant grows each day.

- Your kinesthetic child will enjoy creating the bag.
- Watching the growth of the seeds will help your visual learner to understand the changes seeds go through during germination.
- Your auditory learner may need to verbalize her observations to you.

Mastery occurs when: your child notices the changes that occur as the seeds germinate and she records her observations.

You may want to help your child a little more if: she is having trouble recording observations. Give her a magnifying glass and have her look very closely for any changes. Ask your child to verbalize her observations to you before writing them down.

3 First-Class Classification

Learning happens when: your child develops ways to classify the buttons. Give him the collection of mismatched buttons. Tell your child to figure out a way to put the buttons into groups. Buttons that go together in a group need to be put on a paper plate. There are many ways your child can classify the buttons: by color, by

TIME: 10–15 minutes

MATERIALS
- large collection of mismatched buttons, at least 15–20
- paper plates

how many holes are in the button, by shape, by size, and so on. Once your child has figured out one way, ask him to think of another.

Variations: You can also use seashells, leaves, stamps, baseball cards, and so on. There is really no limit to the number of collections that can be classified in some way.

- Having the buttons to manipulate will help your kinesthetic learner much more than classifying pictures.
- Having the plates available to organize the buttons will help your child visualize the different categories.
- Ask your child to discuss observations about the buttons with you before he starts classifying.

Mastery occurs when: your child can classify the buttons in at least two different ways.

You may want to help your child a little more if: he is having trouble putting the buttons into groups. Ask your child to tell you what he notices about the buttons. He may tell you that they have holes, that they are different colors, that some are plain and some have designs, and so on. Have your child classify the buttons by whatever he notices about them.

4 Data Hunt

TIME: 20 minutes

MATERIALS
- newspapers
- magazines

Learning happens when: you ask your child to look for tables, charts, and graphs in newspapers and magazines and discuss them with your child. Ask her to tell you the purpose of each one. What information is the graph trying to communicate? Why do we even have charts, tables, and graphs? Your child should realize that the purpose of these tools is to organize and communicate information quickly and clearly.

Variations: Ask your child to make up a quiz about the information in a table, graph, or chart to give to you. Tell her that she must ask real questions about the information contained in the graph and must make an answer key to grade your quiz. Take the quiz with all sincerity, asking for your child to clarify a question, if necessary. She will love testing you and will enjoy giving you a grade. After your child has graded the quiz, have a discussion with her about the questions she asked and the questions she could have asked.

- Ask your child to point to bars on a bar graph, tracing them with her finger to see which bar is highest. Tracing the slices in a pie graph or the line in a line graph may give your learner a better sense of which parts of the graph hold more weight.

- The visual clues provided by a table or graph will help your child understand the information much better than just the words and numbers.

- Ask your child to discuss each graph with you in detail and quiz you about it aloud.

Mastery occurs when: your child can tell you what information the chart, graph, or table is trying to convey.

You may want to help your child a little more if: she is having trouble understanding the graph, chart, or table. A graph from a newspaper or a magazine could easily be about something with which your child has had no experience. Make sure it shows information about which your child has some knowledge. Graphs about popular culture or sports probably will appeal to your child more than graphs about the political beliefs of various groups.

Daily Temperature

TIME: 5 minutes
each day

MATERIALS
▪ graph paper
▪ colored pencils or
markers
▪ outdoor thermometer
with Celsius scale
▪ ruler

Prepare the graph paper by writing the days of the week along the bottom of the graph. Along the side of the graph, write the temperature scale in degrees Celsius.

Learning happens when: your child reads a Celsius thermometer daily and records the temperatures on a line graph. At a specific time each day, have your child read the thermometer in degrees Celsius. Once he has found the temperature, he should plot it on the graph by drawing a large dot at the intersection of the line for the current day and the line for the current temperature. Have your child do the same thing the next day, and use a ruler to connect today's dot with yesterday's dot. Continue, and your child will have created a line graph that will show the temperature fluctuations. If he does this for an extended period of time, he will see trends in the temperatures according to season, and he will begin to develop an understanding of the Celsius temperature scale.

Variations: It may be interesting for your child to use the same line graph for Fahrenheit and Celsius temperatures. Ask him to record the Fahrenheit temperature in one color and the Celsius temperature in a different color.

✍ Completing this task daily will give your kinesthetic learner a deeper understanding of how to read a thermometer and the relationships between the temperature and how hot or cold it feels.

👁 Your child will enjoy watching the line graph grow as this activity is completed and will benefit from being able to see the changes in temperature on the graph.

🎧 Engage your child in additional discussion to help him understand the task.

Mastery occurs when: your child can read a thermometer and record the temperature on a line graph.

You may want to help your child a little more if: he is having trouble reading the thermometer or plotting the temperature on the line graph. If your child is having trouble reading the temperature, make sure he understands how the scale of the thermometer is set up. There are many lines that are not labeled. Read the thermometer with your child for several days until he understands how to do it. If your child is having trouble plotting the temperature on the graph, make sure he understands that the dot should be placed on the intersection of two lines: the day line and the temperature line. Again, do this activity with your child for several days until he understands how to do it.

6 | Animal Classification

Learning happens when: your child cuts out pictures of animals from magazines and glues them to index cards. Your child's task is to classify the animals in some way that makes sense and arrange the cards according to the classifications. After your child has classified them and has explained the classification system to you, ask her to classify the animals in a different way. See how many ways your child can classify the animals, such as carnivores or herbivores, four legs or two legs, mammals or egg layers, warm-blooded or cold-blooded, nocturnal or diurnal, and so on.

Variations: Have your child classify the animals in more than two groups at a time, such as forest dwellers, desert dwellers, or water dwellers; walkers, fliers, or swimmers; and so on.

TIME: 15–20 minutes

MATERIALS
- rounded-edge scissors
- magazines with pictures of animals (or buy animal cards made for this purpose)
- nontoxic glue
- index cards

✍ Physically moving the cards will help your kinesthetic learner.

👁 Being able to look at the animals in the various groups will help your child.

👂 Encourage your child to think aloud as she classifies the animals.

Mastery occurs when: your child can classify the animals in more than one way.

You may want to help your child a little more if: she is having trouble understanding how to classify the animals. Keep it simple at first, such as classification by number of legs. As your child gets more comfortable with simple classifications, make it a little more difficult. You may need to have some reference sources available so that your child can look up information about the animals.

7 | Leaf Classification

TIME: 20–30 minutes

MATERIALS
▪ several leaf samples

Learning happens when: your child collects leaves from many different types of trees. After your child has several leaves, have him put them into groups by different attributes, such as shape, size, smooth or serrated edges, and so on. Your child will probably classify the leaves in ways you would never consider. As long as he has consistently classified them in a sensible way, accept his system.

Variations: If your child really enjoyed this activity, ask him to make a leaf book. Attach leaves that belong to the same group to sheets of paper in one section of a notebook. Have a second section for leaves that belong to a second group. Continue for as many groups as are necessary. As your child finds more leaves, he can add them to the book.

☝ Your child will enjoy collecting the leaves and handling them as he classifies them.

👁 Your visual learner will benefit from seeing the leaves grouped in different categories and will enjoy making a notebook.

👂 Ask your child to discuss the things he notices about the leaves before classifying them.

Mastery occurs when: your child can classify the leaves in a way that makes sense.

You may want to help your child a little more if: he is having difficulty classifying the leaves. Ask your child to describe what he notices about the leaves. Build upon what he sees. Ask your child to find one group that is the same in some way. Once your child has made one group, ask him to look at the leftover leaves. Is there some way in which these leaves are alike?

Science Concepts

Third grade science concepts come from physical science, life science, and earth science. In physical science, your child will learn about basic systems and subsystems, as well as how sound is produced and travels. In life science, your child will learn about organisms and their basic needs, characteristics, and habitats. In earth science, your child will learn about forces that change the earth, such as earthquakes and glaciers.

Physical Science

Your child will be studying systems and subsystems. A system is anything that is made up of parts that work together to do something. A very simple system may be a pair of scissors: both sides of a pair of scissors work together to cut things. Some systems are very complex and have numerous subsystems that work together. A car and a bicycle are complex systems made of many subsystems, such as the gear system and the brake system.

In addition to systems, your child will be studying sound. There are five main ideas about sound that he needs to understand.

1. Sound is produced when an object vibrates.

2. The sound of a person talking is the result of that person's vocal cords vibrating. Ask your child to put his hand on the top of his throat while talking—he can feel the vibrations!

3. Sound travels as a wave.

4. Sound waves can be transmitted through solids, liquids, and gases. This concept can be demonstrated in the bathtub. The next time your child takes a bath, have him knock on the side of the tub. When your child is sitting up in the tub, the sound waves are traveling through a gas (the air). Now have him put his ear on the tub as he knocks. The sound waves are traveling through a solid (the bathtub). Finally, ask your child to go under the water and knock on the tub. The sound waves are traveling through a liquid (the bathwater).

5. Sound can be collected and amplified (made louder). A microphone and speakers is an example of a system that collects and amplifies sound. A simple megaphone also amplifies sound.

The table on page 149 describes some important skills related to physical science, where children can run into problems, and what you can do to help them along.

Physical Science Skills	Having Problems?	Quick Tips
Understands the concepts of systems and subsystems.	Does not understand the difference between a system and a subsystem.	Household appliances are great examples of systems. Search the house for systems. Examine some of them to find subsystems. For example, the vacuum is a system. The cord, along with its connections, is a subsystem. The brush and belt work together in another subsystem, and so on.
Understands that sound results when an object vibrates.	Does not understand that sound is a vibration.	Large speakers move because of the vibration of the sound. Put a paper clip on a drum and lightly tap the drum with a drumstick. The paper clip moves because of the vibration. Have your child hold a piece of paper up to his mouth. Make sure the paper is lightly touching the child's lips and that his lips are slightly open. Have your child hum. He should be able to feel the paper softly vibrate because of the sound.

Physical Science Activities

1 A Closer Look at a Bike

Learning happens when: you and your child examine his bicycle. Tell your child that he is going to examine his bicycle to see how it works. Explain that the bike is a system. A system is made of parts that work together to accomplish something. Ask your child to explain the purpose of the bicycle. He should be able to tell you that it is used to get from one place to another. Tell your child that

TIME: 10–15 minutes

MATERIALS
bicycle

the bicycle does many things. There is a subsystem for each thing the bike does. For example, what is the subsystem that makes the bike go? Your child should be able to tell you that pedaling makes the bike go. Have him examine the pedals. What are they attached to? How do they make the wheels turn? Which wheel turns in order to make the bike move? Examine other subsystems, such as the braking subsystem and the steering subsystem.

Variations: You and your child can examine almost anything to see how it works. Use a screwdriver to open a mechanical toy to see how it works. Make sure it's something that can be put back together easily.

- Your child will love manipulating the parts to see what they do and how they work together.

- Seeing how the parts work together will help your visual learner understand systems and subsystems.

- Ask your child to discuss what he sees.

Mastery occurs when: your child can see how the parts of a bicycle's system work together in subsystems to make the bicycle work.

You may want to help your child a little more if: he is having trouble understanding how the parts work together. Turn the bike upside down to see how the pedals and chain work together to turn the wheels. Let your child experiment. Provide guidance as needed, but allow him to figure out as much as possible on his own.

2 A Music Box System

Learning occurs when: your child examines the parts of a music box to see how they work together in a system. Carefully open the music box to see the parts that make the box play music. You may need a small screwdriver to get into the music box. Have your child wind the music box. Ask her to closely examine the system to see how the music plays. There will probably be a system of gears that turn a metal drum on which there are small metal bumps. As the drum turns, the metal bumps go through a system of metal "fingers" that look similar to a comb. It is these fingers plucking the bumps that make the sound.

TIME: 20 minutes

MATERIALS
wind-up music box
small screwdriver

Variations: Ask your child to draw a basic sketch of the system.

- Kinesthetic learners love taking things apart, so this activity will appeal to them.

- Seeing the system at work will help your visual learner understand it better.

- Your child will be interested to find out how the music is produced.

Mastery occurs when: your child understands how the parts work together to create music.

You may want to help your child a little more if: she is having trouble understanding how the system works. Make sure your child understands that a system is simply parts working together to do something. Be very deliberate in looking at the music box system. Look at the key that winds it. What happens when the key is turned? Follow the path in the music box that ultimately leads to the production of music.

3 | Toy System Hunt

TIME: 15–20 minutes

MATERIALS

▪ toys

Learning occurs when: your child finds toys that have a system. Many of your child's toys are made of systems. All of the electronic toys have systems. Even little cars have systems (the wheels, the body, and so on). Ask your child to find at least two examples of toys that have a system. After he has found two toys, ask him to describe the parts and the purpose of each system.

Variations: Ask your child to hunt for other items around the house that have systems. He will find numerous things.

- Your kinesthetic learner will benefit from seeing physical examples of different systems.

- Your visual learner will benefit from seeing how the parts of the system work together to do something.

- Ask your child to discuss the systems he found.

Mastery occurs when: your child can find items that have a system and can tell the parts and function of the system.

You may want to help your child a little more if: he is unsure about which toys have systems and which do not. Ask him to find a toy that does something. For example, it can be a toy that plays music or moves in some way. After your child has found a toy that does something, discuss the parts of the system. Finally, the function of the system is simply what the system is supposed to do. Ask your child to tell you what the toy is supposed to do. After you have discussed a couple of toys with your child, ask him to find another example of a toy with a system, tell you the parts of that system, and tell you what the system is supposed to do.

4 Straw Flute

Learning happens when: your child creates an instrument out of a drinking straw. Have her chew one end of the straw until it is flat. Cut the edges of the flattened end of the straw to make a point. Have your child chew again on the pointed end of the straw to flatten it; however, make sure there is still a narrow gap through which air can be blown. Slightly curl the tips of the points out away from the straw. Have your child put the straw into her mouth and blow a steady, firm stream of air. Your child may need to experiment to make sound. She may need to adjust how far to put the straw into her mouth, how much air to blow, how flat the end needs to be, and so on. The straw instrument will make a definite, strong sound. Ask your child how the straw instrument creates sound. Explain that sound is produced when an object vibrates. Ask her what is vibrating. Your child should realize the pointed ends are vibrating.

Variations: Your child can make a straw trombone with two straws. One straw needs to be slightly larger than the other. Ask her to prepare the first straw as already indicated. Then thread the other straw into the prepared straw. Blow air into the prepared straw, moving the other straw in and out to change the pitch.

✋ Your kinesthetic learner will learn from the vibration on her lips as she blows into the straw.

👁 Your child may want to write down what she did and what happened in a small journal.

👂 Your child will love hearing the results of the vibrating straw.

TIME: 5–10 minutes

MATERIALS
- drinking straw
- rounded-edge scissors

Mastery occurs when: your child can play the straw instrument and understand that the sound comes from the vibration of the straw.

You may want to help your child a little more if: she is having trouble making sound with the straw. Help your child adjust the amount of straw in her mouth and/or the amount of air being blown into the straw. If she is still having trouble, make sure the cut end is not too flat. There needs to be a narrow opening so that air can travel through the straw.

5 Spoon Gong

TIME: 5–10 minutes

MATERIALS
- stainless steel spoon
- rubber band
- 3 feet of string

Learning happens when: your child experiments with the sound created by tapping a spoon on a hard surface. Have your child wrap the handle of the spoon several times with the rubber band, until there is a small loop of rubber band left. Put the string through the little loop so that the spoon is hanging down from the middle of the string with the bowl end pointing downward. Hold one end of the string in each hand. Wrap the ends of the string a couple times around your child's index fingers. Be careful that the string is not too tight. Have your child bend slightly at the waist and put his index fingers in his ears. The spoon should be hanging down with no slack in the string. Have your child gently swing the spoon so that it taps something hard and listen to the sound it makes. This is an example of sound traveling through a solid. The sound travels from the spoon, to the rubber band, to the string, to your child's fingers, and finally to his ears.

Variations: Try other eating utensils, such as a fork or a butter knife. What kind of sound do those items make?

✋ Doing this experiment will help your child understand how

sound travels and how different the sound is when heard through the string instead of through the air.

👁 Your visual learner may want to make notes about the experiment and the results.

👂 Your child will be amazed at how different the sound is through the string.

Mastery occurs when: your child realizes that the sound is traveling through a solid (the string), which sounds different from the sound traveling through the air.

You may want to help your child a little more if: he is having difficulty hearing the sound. Make sure there is no slack in the string. Also make sure that the spoon is hanging down from the string.

6 | Supersound Cone

Learning happens when: your child uses a supersound cone to collect and amplify sounds. Roll the poster board into a cone shape, leaving a hole about the size of a dime at the pointed end. Leave the other end as wide as you can. Tape the edges to keep the poster board in the cone shape. Have your child take the cone outside and put the small end up to her ear. (Be careful that she does not stick the cone into the ear canal.) Have your child point the cone in different directions and listen carefully. She should be able to hear sounds that are too soft to hear without the cone.

Variations: Make a megaphone with the poster board. Make the hole at the pointed end a little larger. Take your child outside. Stand far apart and experiment with talking and shouting with and without the cone. Switch roles so that each of you can hear the difference in sound with the megaphone.

TIME: 10–15 minutes

MATERIALS
- poster board, about 18 × 24 inches
- tape

Have your child help you make the supersound cone.

Ask your child to write down her observations in a science journal.

This and other sound experiments will naturally appeal to your auditory learner.

Mastery occurs when: your child can connect listening through the supersound cone with the concept of collecting and amplifying sound.

You may want to help your child a little more if: she cannot hear the difference between sounds with and without using the sound cone. Make sure the poster board is cone-shaped, with a small pointed end and a large bell-shaped end. Make sure your child is holding the pointed end up to her ear. If she can hear the difference but cannot explain it, ask your child if she can hear better with or without the sound cone. Why can she hear better? Your child should understand that she can hear better because the sound is collected and amplified by the sound cone.

7 | Chicken in a Cup

TIME: 20–30 minutes

MATERIALS
- 1 foot of string
- paper clip
- paper cup
- water

Learning happens when: your child ties one end of the string around the paper clip. Have him poke a small hole in the bottom of the paper cup. Then have your child turn the cup upside down and thread the other end of the string through the bottom of the cup so that the string is hanging down inside the cup (similar to a bell). The paper clip will prevent the string from going completely through the hole. Have your child hold the cup upside down in one hand and grasp the string. Then have him pull the string in firm, jerking motions. He should be pulling hard enough that his hand is moving slightly down the string with each jerking motion. Note the sound made. Now have him wet the string and do the same thing. The water changes the sound, so it should now be loud and resemble a clucking chicken. What is happening? By pulling the string, your child is causing it to vibrate. The sound waves move through the string, to the paper clip, and finally to the cup. The cup serves to collect and amplify the sound waves, which makes a loud sound.

Variations: Try this with different cup sizes. Is the sound different depending on the size and shape of the cup? How is the sound different with a plastic cup? Ask your child to experiment with different types of cups and keep notes on his observations.

- Your child will enjoy creating and experiencing different sounds.

- Encourage your child to decorate his cup to look like a chicken.

- This project will help your child understand how sound is made and how it is amplified.

Mastery occurs when: your child understands that pulling the string is causing the string to vibrate, the sound waves travel through the string to the cup, and the cup collects and amplifies the sound.

You may want to help your child a little more if: he is having trouble making the sound. Make sure the string is wet. Also, make sure your child is holding the string firmly and pulling down in short, jerking motions.

Life Science

Within the area of life science, your child will be studying the basic needs, characteristics, and habitats of living things. He will learn that all living organisms have basic needs. Having a pet provides a wonderful lesson in the characteristics, needs, and habitats of organisms. If you do not provide for your pet's basic needs, your pet will get sick and/or die. Ask your child to list some of the needs of a pet. He should be able to tell you a pet needs food, water, and shelter.

In addition to basic needs, your child will also learn how different characteristics help animals survive in different habitats. For example, a fawn's hide camouflages the baby deer in the forest. If the fawn were

Life Science Skills	Having Problems?	Quick Tips
Understands that all living things have basic needs.	Does not understand the basic needs of organisms.	Discuss the things your child needs to survive. Then discuss the things a pet needs to survive. Finally, discuss the things other animals need to survive. Your child should see that there are certain things that all living things need to survive.
Understands that certain characteristics of animals help them to survive.	Does not understand that there are characteristics that help animals survive.	Read books about animals and plants that live in extreme environments, such as the desert or the arctic. Emphasize characteristics that help those organisms survive in such harsh conditions.
Understands that a habitat must meet the needs of the organisms that live there.	Does not understand that a habitat must support the needs of its organisms.	Read books about animals living in extreme conditions, then talk to your child about what would happen if one of those animals were moved to a different place. For example, what would happen if a polar bear were moved to the desert?

moved to a different habitat, however, such as the arctic, the fawn would be easy to spot. Another example is the cactus. It is designed to live in arid climates. If a cactus is planted in a swamp, it will not survive because it is not designed to live in wet areas.

Another concept your child will learn about is the food chain and how organisms are interdependent in the food chain: disturbances in one area of the food chain affect all other areas. Your child will learn how habitats change over time and how one habitat can be gradually replaced by another. The table on page 158 describes some important skills related to life science, where children can run into problems, and what you can do to help them along.

Life Science Activities

1 Habitat Succession

Learning happens when: your child is able to see in miniature how a wet habitat can gradually change to a forested habitat. Have him place 2 inches of soil and 3 inches of water in the jar. Leave the open jar on a windowsill overnight. The next day, plant an aquatic plant in the jar. It should grow well. Do not replace the water as it evaporates. After a few days, and then once or twice a week, have your child add three or four birdseeds to the jar. While the water is in the jar, the seeds should germinate and then rot. As the water evaporates, the aquatic plant will die. Continue adding birdseeds, even after the water has evaporated. The seeds will now find an environment suitable for growth. Sunflower seeds can be added to represent trees. Your child will now need to add water, as a substitute for rainfall, in order for the "forest" to continue growing.

Variations: Ask your child to follow up with a poster showing how his pond habitat changed to a forest habitat.

TIME: 5 minutes each day

MATERIALS
- soil
- water
- quart jar
- aquatic plants
- 2 cups of birdseed

✋ Completing this experiment will help your kinesthetic learner understand how habitats change over time.

👁 Your visual learner may enjoy the variation of creating a poster.

👂 Your auditory learner will benefit from discussing what is happening.

Mastery occurs when: your child understands that habitats can change over time.

You may want to help your child a little more if: he is having trouble understanding why the aquatic plant is no longer growing but the seeds are. Discuss what changes took place over time in the jar. Your child should be able to tell you that the water disappeared. When the water was in the jar, the aquatic plant did well, but the seeds did not do well. When the water evaporated, the aquatic plant did not do well, but the seeds did do well. Ask him to verbalize how much water was needed for the seeds to be successful and for the aquatic plant to be successful.

2 Food Chain

TIME: 10–15 minutes

MATERIALS
- index cards
- markers
- stopwatch

Prepare the cards by writing the names of organisms in a food chain that eat other organisms—for example, grass, mouse, snake, and hawk.

Learning happens when: your child puts the cards in order to show the food chain. Turn the cards facedown and get the stopwatch ready. Have your child turn the cards over and put them in order of who eats what, as quickly as possible. (In the example here, the grass is eaten by the mouse, which is eaten by the snake, which is eaten by the hawk.)

Variations: Ask your child to research food chains to create her own set of cards. There are many concepts within the food chain, such as herbivores (plant eaters) tend to be at the bottom of the food chain, while carnivores (meat eaters) tend to be at the top. Ask your child to read books about the food chain, sharing interesting facts or thoughts with you.

- Moving the cards around will help your kinesthetic learner work through the food chain.

- Seeing the different food-chain combinations that can be made will help your child choose the correct sequence.

- Have your auditory learner say what's going on in the food chain.

Mastery occurs when: your child understands that animals in the food chain are interdependent. For example, if disease kills many mice one year, the snakes will be affected because the snakes' food source will be smaller. Fewer snakes will survive due to a lack of food, and the hawks will be affected because there will be fewer snakes to eat.

You may want to help your child a little more if: she is having trouble understanding the food chain. Start with three cards. Once your child is successful with three cards, try four.

3 Animal Cards

TIME: 45–60 minutes

MATERIALS
- reference books about animals
- index cards
- markers, crayons, pencils

Learning happens when: your child researches animals and creates a system of animal cards. Have him check out several books about animals from the local library. Tell your child that he will be making animal cards similar to baseball cards. On the front, have him write the name of the animal, then draw and color a picture of the animal. On the back, your child should write the vital statistics of the animal, such as its size, what it eats, where it lives, how long it lives, and how many offspring it has. Have him make several different animal cards.

Variations: Your child can create animal cards for various habitat "teams." For example, for the team "Forest Rangers," your child could do animal cards with the animals from a forest habitat. For the team "Desert Dodgers," your child could do a set of desert animal cards.

Your child will enjoy making and working with the animal cards in groups.

Your visual learner will benefit from seeing the cards grouped together by habitat and may work very hard to make sure his animal cards are visually pleasing and similar in format.

Your auditory learner may need to talk about what he will put on the card.

Mastery occurs when: your child can tell you the characteristics and habitats of the animals for which cards have been made.

You may want to help your child a little more if: he is having trouble finding the information. Make sure the reference book is not too difficult. If it is, look for books that are easier to read. If your child enjoys working on the computer, have him conduct the research online or through an encyclopedia CD.

4   Find the Food Chain

TIME: 30 minutes

MATERIALS
- index cards
- markers
- reference books about animals

Learning happens when: your child works backward to find the food chain. There are many predators that intrigue children. Have your child pick her favorite predator, such as a hawk. Ask her to find out one thing that the predator eats. (The hawk eats a bird.) Then have your child research one thing that that animal eats. (The bird eats a grasshopper.) Then research one thing that that animal eats. (The grasshopper eats grass.) Your child has found the beginning of the food chain when she finds a plant. Have her write each member of the food chain on index cards, using one color of ink. Ask your child to do the same thing with a different predator. Write those members of the food chain on index cards, using a different color. After finding the food chain for several predators, she should realize all food chains begin with plants. Plants are called producers because they make their own food through photosynthesis. Animals cannot make their own food, so they must get it from other sources. Herbivores use plants for food. Carnivores use animals for food.

Variations: Using drawings of each animal or plant, ask your child to make a poster of the various food chains.

✋ Arranging the cards will benefit your kinesthetic learner.

👁 Your child will enjoy making the poster.

👂 Discuss the food chain with your child so that she will understand how it works.

Mastery occurs when: your child understands that living things depend on other living things for food and that the food chain begins with plants, which are producers.

You may want to help your child a little more if: she is having trouble figuring out the food chain. Help her to be very deliberate and organized in her research. You may need to help your child research the animals.

5 Design a Habitat

TIME: 30–45 minutes

MATERIALS
■ shoebox
■ basic craft supplies, such as markers, construction paper, nontoxic glue, rounded-edge scissors, etc.

Learning happens when: your child chooses an animal and creates a diorama of a habitat suitable for that animal—that is, it must meet the needs of the organism living there. The habitat must provide five things: food, water, air, space, and shelter. To create a diorama, your child should turn the shoebox on its side and create a scene inside the box. You may want to write the five things the habitat must have on a piece of paper. As your child creates the diorama, have him cross the five things off the list as they are included.

Variations: Your child can draw a picture or make a poster of a suitable habitat for his animal.

🖐 Creating a habitat will help your kinesthetic learner think about how the habitat meets the needs of the animal.

👁 This is a good project for your visual learner just the way it is.

👂 Ask your child to discuss how his habitat meets the needs of the animal.

Mastery occurs when: your child has created a habitat that meets the five needs of his animal and can explain how the habitat meets those needs.

You may want to help your child a little more if: he did not include all five needs of the animal. Ask him to show you where the animal will get food. If the animal eats insects, your child needs to include insects in the diorama. Ask him to show you where the animal will find shelter. Continue asking questions until all the animal's needs are met.

6 Which Category?

TIME: 15–20 minutes

MATERIALS
- 15 index cards
- pencils
- 3 paper plates

Write the following producers on five index cards: grass, fern, daisy, rose, and cucumber. Write the following herbivores on five index cards: grasshopper, mouse, cow, deer, and horse. Write the following carnivores on five index cards: frog, snake, bird, fox, and wolf. Write "Producers" on one paper plate, "Herbivores" on a second paper plate, and "Carnivores" on a third paper plate.

Learning happens when: your child divides the index cards into three groups. Explain the groups to her. Producers are organisms that make their own food through photosynthesis. Plants are the only living things that can make their own food. Herbivores are organisms that eat only plants for food. Carnivores are organisms that eat other animals for food. Mix up the index cards, and have your child put the index cards on the correct plates. If your child is competitive, have her race the clock to see how quickly she can classify the organisms.

Variations: Ask your child to make her own set of cards for you to categorize. Make sure she makes an answer key. Compare your answers to her answer key. If the answers do not match, research with your child to determine the proper category for that organism.

✍ Your child will enjoy moving the cards into the proper groups.

👁 Allow your child to make her own cards.

Your child may need to think aloud as she categorizes the organisms.

Mastery occurs when: your child knows what each category means and can put the organisms into the proper category.

You may want to help your child a little more if: she is having trouble categorizing the cards. Make sure she knows what the categories mean. Then ask her to tell you what the organism eats. If your child does not know what the organism eats, she may need to do more research.

7 | Animal Awards

TIME: 60 minutes

MATERIALS
- reference books about animals
- markers
- construction paper
- nontoxic glue
- rounded-edge scissors

Learning occurs when: your child researches animals and gives awards based on the characteristics of the animals. Have him think of some awards to give animals—for example, Best Camouflage, Most Unique Defense, Fastest Animal, Loudest Animal, Most Unique Talent, Most Poisonous, and so on. Have your child research animals to determine the recipients of the awards. Using markers, construction paper, glue, and scissors, ask him to make ribbons or awards for those animals.

Variations: If your child loves to do things in a big way, have him make up an awards show. Record your child's show with a video camera.

Your child will enjoy creating the awards.

Your visual learner will want to make sure his awards are eye-catching. You can give him extra materials, such as glitter or stickers, to decorate the awards.

Your child will enjoy recording the awards show.

Mastery occurs when: your child discovers that animals have unique characteristics that help them survive.

You may want to help your child a little more if: he is having trouble finding an animal for an award. Have him research an animal and design an award for that animal based on its unique characteristics.

Earth Science

In addition to studying physical science and life science, your child will be studying earth science. Specifically, she will be looking at the forces that shape the earth. These forces include glaciers, earthquakes, volcanoes, and erosion. For example, the rounded shape of the Appalachian Mountains was caused by the movement of glaciers millions of years ago. The Appalachians contrast sharply with the jagged peaks of the Rocky Mountains. The Grand Canyon was formed mostly by water erosion. Earthquakes can change the landscape in ten seconds. Finally, volcanoes have changed the earth by creating islands such as Hawaii. The following table describes some important skills related to earth science, where children can run into problems, and what you can do to help them along.

Earth Science Skills	Having Problems?	Quick Tips
Understands that the earth is constantly changing.	Thinks that the earth does not change.	Research natural disasters with your child. Find before and after pictures of places that have been affected by a natural disaster such as an earthquake, a tornado, or a hurricane.
Understands some of the forces that change the earth.	Does not know how the earth is changed.	Find books about natural disasters. Many third graders enjoy reading about tornadoes and earthquakes. Your child can also find books about the Grand Canyon and the Hawaiian Islands that explain how the canyon and the islands were formed.

Earth Science Activities

1 Cake Pan Earthquake

TIME: 15–20 minutes

MATERIALS

▪ 2 strips of plastic or cloth
▪ cake pan
▪ damp soil
▪ toy houses, cars, etc.

Learning happens when: your child simulates an earthquake. The earth's crust is made of plates that float on a bed of hot, molten rock. When the plates rub together, an earthquake occurs. Have your child put the two strips of plastic or cloth on the bottom of the cake pan. They should be arranged next to each other, with the excess length of the strips hanging over opposite ends of the cake pan. Have your child cover the strips with damp soil to the edge of the pan and pack the soil down firmly. He can then place toys to represent houses, cars, buildings, and so on, on top of the soil. Ask him to hold one plastic strip and you hold the other. Simultaneously pull on the strips. Ask your child to describe what happens.

Variations: Ask your child to research why earthquakes cause so much destruction, what types of buildings are best able to withstand an earthquake, and how to stay safe during an earthquake.

🖐 Your child will enjoy creating an earthquake.

👁 Seeing how the toys are affected by the moving soil will help your visual learner understand the basics of an earthquake.

👂 Have your auditory learner describe what is happening during the earthquake and why.

Mastery occurs when: your child can describe what happens in the simulated earthquake and can predict what may happen in a real earthquake.

You may want to help your child a little more if: he cannot extend this activity to what may happen in a real earthquake. There are many wonderful, kid-friendly Web sites that teach about earthquakes.

2 Car Seismograph

Learning occurs when: your child learns how a seismograph works by simulating one in the car. A seismograph is a machine that is used to measure the vibrations within the earth and on the ground. It is also used to measure the severity of an earthquake. This activity works best with a road that is mildly bumpy. Clip a piece of paper to the clipboard. Have your child hold the clipboard in one hand on her knees. With the other hand, she should hold a pen at arm's length so that it touches the paper. While the car is moving, have your child move the pen very slowly from left to right. At the end of the ride, have her look at the results. Was the line smooth? What caused the line to jump up or down? A seismograph works in a similar way. Instead of measuring bumps in the road, it measures movement of the earth.

Variations: Ask your child to make a seismograph reading on different roads and compare the results. Do different roads have very different readings?

- Your kinesthetic learner will enjoy going over the bumps and being able to hold the seismograph.
- Seeing the results will help your visual learner understand how a seismograph records vibrations.
- Ask your child to discuss her findings with you.

TIME: 10–15 minutes

MATERIALS
- clipboard
- paper
- pens

3 Working Volcano

Learning happens when: your child creates a volcano and observes how the lava flows. First, make the salt dough, which will be used to form the volcano. Mix the flour, salt, cooking oil, and water in

TIME: 45 minutes

MATERIALS

- 6 cups of flour
- 2 cups of salt
- 4 tablespoons of cooking oil
- 2 cups of water
- empty soda bottle
- baking pan
- warm water
- 2 drops of red food coloring
- 6 drops of liquid dish detergent
- 2 tablespoons of baking soda
- 2 cups of vinegar

a large bowl. Knead with your hands until the mixture can be manipulated into shapes. Add a little more water if the mixture is too dry. Place the soda bottle upright in the baking pan. Have your child use the salt dough to make a volcano shape around the soda bottle, making sure the mouth of the bottle is not covered and no dough is dropped into the bottle. After he has made the volcano, have him carefully pour warm water into the bottle until it is two-thirds full. Add the red food coloring and liquid detergent to the bottle. Add the baking soda. Slowly pour the vinegar into the bottle while standing back because a reaction will occur fairly quickly. Have your child observe how the lava flows down the volcano. Tell him that lava is melted rock. Eventually, the lava will harden. Ask your child if the landscape would be changed after a volcanic eruption.

Variations: Sometimes a volcanic eruption is more explosive than this experiment shows. You can create a more explosive volcano, but it's best to set it off outside. Prepare the volcano as already stated. Then fill the bottle about halfway with equal parts warm water, food coloring, and vinegar. Add the liquid detergent. Wrap a couple of tablespoons of baking soda in a paper towel. When you are ready for the eruption, drop the paper towel–wrapped baking soda into the bottle, put a cork in the mouth of the bottle, and stand back. In a few moments, the volcanic eruption will shoot the cork into the air.

- Your child will enjoy all the steps of creating the volcano— making the dough, shaping the volcano, pouring the liquids, and so on.

- Your visual learner will get a better understanding of how volcanoes shape the earth by seeing the lava flow down the sides of the volcano.

Encourage your child to talk about what happened.

Mastery occurs when: your child understands how lava flows out of an erupting volcano and how a volcanic eruption changes the landscape.

You may want to help your child a little more if: he is having trouble understanding how a volcano changes the earth. There are many kid-friendly Web sites designed to teach your child about volcanoes. Do some research with him. Get a book about the Ring of Fire, a ring of active volcanoes in the Pacific Ocean.

4 Tornado Tube

Learning happens when: your child creates a tornado inside the soda bottles. Fill one of the soda bottles almost to the top with water. Turn the other soda bottle upside down, and place it mouth-to-mouth on top of the first soda bottle. Use the duct tape to carefully tape the bottles together by wrapping the tape around the mouths. Make sure the soda bottles are securely connected to each other and do not leak. Have your child swirl the water around, flip the filled bottle upside down, and watch as the water forms a vortex and swirls like a tornado. Explain to her that a tornado occurs when a current of warm air collides with a current of cold air. The currents start to swirl, and if the conditions are right, a vortex forms and the tornado reaches the ground.

TIME: 10–15 minutes

MATERIALS
- 2 two-liter soda bottles, clean and dry
- duct tape
- water

Variations: Add 2 ounces of colored oil or food coloring to create a colored tornado effect.

Your child will enjoy creating a tornado, even if it's just in a bottle.

👁 Seeing the vortex will help your visual learner understand the way air moves in a tornado.

👂 Ask your child to discuss what she sees in the tornado.

Mastery occurs when: your child can locate the vortex and understands that the water is mimicking the movement of air in a tornado.

You may want to help your child a little more if: she cannot create the tornado. Make sure your child is swirling the water, not just shaking it. If she continues to have trouble, experiment with the tornado tube to see if you can create a tornado.

5 | Safety Posters

TIME: Varies

MATERIALS
▪ reference books about natural disasters
▪ poster board
▪ markers

Learning happens when: your child researches how to stay safe during a tornado, earthquake, or volcanic eruption. Once your child has researched the subject, have him make a safety poster that tells kids what they should do in each event.

Variation: If your child loves to be on camera, he can create a public service announcement.

✋ Ask your child to act out what to do during these events.

👁 Your child will enjoy and learn from making a poster.

👂 Your aural learner may enjoy making a public service announcement more than making a poster.

Mastery occurs when: your child can tell you what safety precautions need to be taken in the event of a tornado, an earthquake, or a volcanic eruption.

You may want to help your child a little more if: he is having trouble with the research. Go to the library with him. Look in the nonfiction children's section for books on volcanoes, tornadoes, and earthquakes. Help him use the index of a reference book to find safety precautions for each of these events.

6 Erosion

Learning happens when: your child sees how erosion occurs in miniature form. Have her fill the baking tray with soil and pat down firmly. Scatter a few rocks on the soil and embed them so that they do not move. The rocks need to be large enough that they will not be covered when pushed into the soil. Lift the short end of the baking tray and place it on a book so that the tray is inclined. Have your child carefully pour drops of water onto the top of the tray and observe what happens. Pour a few more drops of water onto the tray and observe. Continue several more times. Have your child write her observations in a journal.

TIME: 20 minutes

MATERIALS
- baking tray
- soil
- rocks
- book
- water
- journal
- pencils

Variations: Put ice cubes on the soil. Observe what happens as the ice cubes melt.

- Creating a small environment in which to observe erosion will help your kinesthetic learner understand it.
- Your visual learner will learn best by seeing what happens when water is added to the tray.
- Encourage your child to discuss her observations.

Mastery occurs when: your child understands that erosion causes some of the soil to be washed away and that the rocks help keep some of the soil in place.

You may want to help your child a little more if: she is having trouble understanding erosion. Ask her to tell you what is happening to the soil as the water is rolling over it. Your child should observe that some of the soil is being washed away. Explain that the soil being washed away is erosion.

 **Erosion Hunt**

TIME: 20–25 minutes

MATERIALS

journal

pencils

Learning occurs when: your child searches an outdoor area for signs of erosion. Tell him that erosion can affect more than just soil. Erosion can affect rocks. For example, river rocks are very smooth because the water constantly runs over them. Erosion can be seen in dirt that has been washed away, in areas around drain pipes, and on the edges of a concrete sidewalk. Have your child bring a small science journal to note signs of erosion. You may be surprised at the amount of things he finds.

Variations: Your child can document signs of erosion on film. If he is a shutterbug, have him take pictures. Alternately, your child may enjoy getting out the video camera.

- Your child will enjoy the hunt.
- Your visual learner will enjoy documenting his findings in a journal.
- Your child may enjoy documenting his findings with a tape recorder.

Mastery occurs when: your child correctly identifies several varied sources of minor erosion.

You may want to help your child a little more if: he doesn't grasp the concept that soil moves and erosion is a big source of that movement. Choose a spot in your yard and mix some colored sand into the topsoil. Observe what happens to the colored sand and soil mixture over the next few days. Where did the colored part go? Talk about how the wind and rain moves soil from one place to another.

Environmental Learning

As always, there are many opportunities to reinforce your child's science skills and knowledge in the everyday world. Practice observation skills at any given opportunity. When you have a fan going, talk into it, then discuss sound vibrations, waves, and amplification. See a turtle on the road? Talk about habitat and species survival. Do whatever you can to relate what your child is learning to the world around him or her.

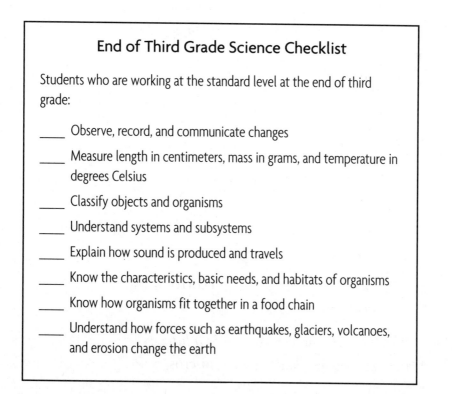

End of Third Grade Science Checklist

Students who are working at the standard level at the end of third grade:

_____ Observe, record, and communicate changes

_____ Measure length in centimeters, mass in grams, and temperature in degrees Celsius

_____ Classify objects and organisms

_____ Understand systems and subsystems

_____ Explain how sound is produced and travels

_____ Know the characteristics, basic needs, and habitats of organisms

_____ Know how organisms fit together in a food chain

_____ Understand how forces such as earthquakes, glaciers, volcanoes, and erosion change the earth

Third Grade Social Studies

9

Social studies, like science, is becoming more prominent in your child's day. Your child will continue to learn about the world around him, and many times the topics he encounters complement the science topics being learned in school. Building on the science skills your child is developing, climates will probably be a focus this year. Map skills fit nicely with climate topics, and your child will also study how people live and the jobs they do in the climates and regions in which they live. A third grader's biggest task is to figure out how all of these things connect to affect people.

Now that your child has learned about his own community, family, school, city, and state, it's time to expand to other communities within the United States and around the world. Your child will learn more in-depth map skills, and geography will play a big role in the social studies curriculum. A new focus will be economics and how money and finances relate to your child's world.

Map Skills

As a second grade student, your child learned what a map is and how to read the map key. The map key usually has several symbols that represent places. A black dot (.) usually means a city; a star (*) usually stands for a state capital. While these two symbols are fairly standard, there are many different symbols for other things on maps. Your child must learn to look at the key in order to read a map.

There are other map skills your child will focus on this year, such as locating the equator and the prime meridian. These are imaginary lines that divide the earth into hemispheres. A hemisphere is a half of the earth.

Map Skills	Having Problems?	Quick Tips
Recognizes map symbols and easily interprets them.	Can't make heads or tails of the map symbols.	Flash cards—we just can't get enough of them. Make some flash cards that have the map symbols on one side and their definitions on the other side.
Locates and identifies parts of a world map, such as the equator and the prime meridian.	Mixes up the equator and the prime meridian.	Draw a line across a sheet of paper and another one that crosses it going up and down (it will look like a big plus sign). Label the line that goes across "equator" and the one that goes up and down "prime meridian."
Understands many kinds of maps.	Can't get past the idea that maps do more than get you from here to there.	Find a map of your state at www.knowledgeessentials.com. Print it out and talk about what the map tells you (the shape of your state). Take the blank state map and ask your child to draw in symbols to represent things that he knows about your state (an X for places where family members live is a good start). Once your child gets the concept from his own map, try reading a population map together.

The equator runs east and west and divides the earth into the northern and southern hemispheres. The prime meridian runs north and south and divides the earth into the eastern and western hemispheres.

Your child will also learn how to read a map grid, making it easier to quickly find places on a map. Another focus will be learning to use the compass rose to determine cardinal and intermediate directions. Cardinal directions are north, south, east, and west. Intermediate directions fall in between cardinal directions: northeast, southeast, northwest, and southwest. These are important skills that will provide your third grader with a good foundation for future studies. The table on page 178 describes some important skills related to maps, where children can run into problems, and what you can do to help them along.

Map Skills Activities

1 Symbol Brainstorm

Learning happens when: you and your child brainstorm a list of places that you might find on a map. After you have this list, have your child brainstorm symbols to represent each type of place—for example, a tree for a forest, a slide for a playground, and an elephant for a zoo. Decide on one symbol for each type of place. List the places on chart paper with their symbols in alphabetical order.

TIME: 20–30 minutes

MATERIALS
- markers
- chart paper (you can buy this, or you can print some out from www .knowledgeessentials.com)

Variations: Instead of chart paper, fold some paper in half and staple it to make a book. Title the book "My Symbols," then ask your child to list the types of places and their symbols in alphabetical order.

Ask your child to put the symbols on index cards and then mix them up. You can then call out an object or a place, such as the forest. Your child should try to find a symbol from the index cards that would best represent that type of place.

👁 This activity is great for your visual learner because it focuses on picture symbols.

👂 Ask your auditory learner to read aloud the name of the type of place as he is drawing or identifying the symbol.

Mastery occurs when: your child can choose objects that make sense in representing something in the real world.

You may want to help your child a little more if: he cannot pick a reasonable symbol to represent a type of place in the real world.

2 Map Making

TIME: 20–30 minutes

MATERIALS
- construction paper
- pencils
- map pencils

Learning happens when: you ask your child to picture her school. Have her write down all the rooms and places she thinks would be important for a visitor to be able to easily find. Then ask her to draw the basic shape of the school on the construction paper. Have her choose a symbol to represent each of the rooms and places—for example, a book for the library and a computer for the computer lab. Then on the basic shape your child drew, have her draw all of the rooms in the school building. Don't forget to include the locations of the parking lot and the playground. Have your child create a key for the map, making sure it is large enough to hold all of the symbols she has chosen. Ask her to put her symbols in the appropriate places on the map.

Variations: Instead of the school, you can have your child draw a map of a shopping mall, a sports complex, or a grocery store.

 It would be a good idea to let your kinesthetic learner walk around the place she will be mapping out and draw a rough draft before she starts the real map. She might want to make some of the map three-dimensional by using folded paper.

 This activity will appeal to visual learners. Your child will also benefit from walking around the place she is going to map. Color coding the map would be beneficial.

Ask your child to make a recording of herself explaining the map and its key.

Mastery occurs when: your child can choose objects that sensibly represent something in the real world.

You may want to help your child a little more if: she cannot pick a reasonable symbol to represent a type of room.

3 United States Travel

Learning happens when: you and your child look at a map of the United States. Tell your child to place a marker on his home state. Then tell him to move his marker to another spot on the map, such as a different state. Ask in which direction he traveled. Continue with this process until you think your child understands cardinal and intermediate directions on the map.

Variations: Write the names of states on index cards. Ask your child to draw a card and move his marker to that state. Ask your child in which direction he moved his marker to get to that state. Ask him what place or thing he would like to see or visit in each state.

Some schools have U.S. maps painted on their playground. This would be perfect for your kinesthetic learner. Instead of using a marker, he can move from state to state himself.

TIME: 20–30 minutes

MATERIALS
- U.S. map (you can print a copy at www .knowledgeessentials.com)
- object to mark your spot (bean, red dot)

- The activity is good for your visual learner because the map is a visual representation of the United States.

- Your auditory learner will do well with this activity because you will be giving him directions orally. Ask him to repeat the directions as he moves the marker from state to state.

Mastery occurs when: your child can identify the correct cardinal and intermediate directions as the marker is moved from state to state.

You may want to help your child a little more if: he cannot identify the correct directions. You might want to do the activity using only the cardinal directions. When your child is successful, add the intermediate directions.

4 | Equator

TIME: 20–30 minutes

MATERIALS
- drawing compass
- paper
- pencil

Learning happens when: your child uses the compass to draw a circle of any size on a piece of paper. Then have her draw a line horizontally across the center of the circle. Label the horizontal line "equator." Explain to your child that the equator divides the earth into the northern hemisphere and the southern hemisphere. Have her label each hemisphere on the map.

Variations: You could also have your child add the continents to the drawing.

- Ask your child to do a three-dimensional version by drawing a line around the middle of some type of ball to show the equator and the hemispheres.

- Repeat each step aloud as your child completes it. If you use a real ball, play a game of catch and ask your child to say the name of the hemisphere that her hands touch first when she catches the ball.

Mastery occurs when: your child can label the equator and the northern and southern hemispheres on a map or globe.

You may want to help your child a little more if: she cannot correctly identify and label the equator and the northern and southern hemispheres. Try having her color the two hemispheres to help identify them.

5 Prime Meridian

Learning happens when: your child uses a piece of chalk to draw a large circle on the sidewalk. Then have him draw a vertical line going through the middle of the entire circle. Your child should label this line "prime meridian." The half of the circle on the left should be labeled "western hemisphere" and the half on the right should be labeled "eastern hemisphere."

TIME: 20–30 minutes

MATERIALS
sidewalk chalk

Variations: You could also have your child add the continents to the drawing.

 Ask your child to make a three-dimensional version by drawing a line around the middle of some type of ball to show the prime meridian and the hemispheres.

Repeat each step aloud as your child completes it. If you use a real ball, play a game of catch and ask your child to say the name of the hemisphere that his hands touch first when he catches the ball.

Mastery occurs when: your child can label the prime meridian and the western and eastern hemispheres on a map or globe.

You may want to help your child a little more if: he cannot correctly identify and label the prime meridian and the western and eastern hemispheres. Try having him color the two hemispheres to help identify them.

6 Product Maps and Symbols

TIME: 20–30 minutes

MATERIALS
▪ state product map (you can find one for each state at www .knowledgeessentials.com)

Learning happens when: you and your child study the product map of your state or any other state that appeals to her. Look at the map key and discuss what each symbol represents. Ask your child questions about the map: What is this state's most popular product? What product is produced closest to where we live?

Variations: You could practice using the cardinal directions (compass rose) with the activity.

Ask your child to gather items around the house that can represent the product symbols used on the map. She can use these as manipulatives when discussing the product map.

Take your visual learner to a store to see the various products. She can design an advertisement for television, a newspaper, or a magazine for the state's products.

Encourage your child to create a radio advertisement for the state's products.

Mastery occurs when: your child can read and understand the product map.

You may want to help your child a little more if: she is having trouble answering your questions about the map. Ask a question, then point out the symbols to her.

7 Using a Grid

Learning happens when: you and your child write the names of
streets and places of interest from your city on the index cards.
Examples of places of interest might be schools, parks, libraries,
shopping malls, or city hall. Have your child close his eyes to pick
an index card, then have him look at the map. Most city maps will
have letters of the alphabet across the top and bottom of the map
and numbers on both sides of the map. Below is an example of a
grid system.

TIME: 20–30 minutes

MATERIALS
city map (one that uses
a grid system)
index cards
pencils

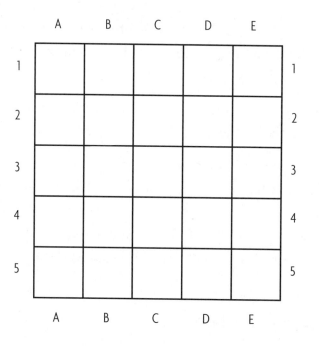

Have your child find the place of interest from the index card on
the map and determine the grid square location. Write the letter
and number of that square—for example, B5—on the other side
of the index card. Continue this procedure on the index cards
with the rest of the places or streets.

Variations: You can give the letter and number to your child first and have him pick out a place of interest in that square.

✋ Ask your child to use his fingers to touch the letter and the number, then pull his fingers in a straight line together until they meet on the grid.

👁 It would be a good idea to take your visual learner on a tour of your town or city before you do this activity. This way he will have a visual perception of where things are in the city.

👂 Your auditory learner can say the letter and number aloud as he finds the correct square. When your child has found the correct square, ask him to repeat the letter and number and the street or place of interest—for example, C3, the city swimming pool.

Mastery occurs when: your child can use the grid system to find the places indicated on the index cards on the map.

You may want to help your child a little more if: he can't find the places you ask using the grid system. Start by having him find places that are in one section of the map. For example, give all of the A combinations first: A1, A2, A3, and so on. Do this until your child has a better understanding of how the grid system works.

8 | Giving Directions

TIME: 20–30 minutes

MATERIALS
- compass
- various objects
- paper
- pencils

Learning happens when: you give your child a compass and ask her to give you directions to an object using the cardinal and intermediate directions. You can establish a rule that your child cannot get to the object by traveling in a straight line. Tell her the object for which you want her to give you directions—for example, the swing set. Determine a starting point for the activity and have your child stand there. Ask her to tell you the first direction and how many steps to go. For example, she might say, "Go four steps to the southwest." Write this down on the paper. Have your child give the next step, such as, "Take ten steps to the north." Write this down. Repeat the procedure until your child arrives at the object. Instead of giving her the object and having her come up with the directions, try giving her directions and see if she can find the object. For example, ask your child to face north. Then tell her to take four steps to the southwest, then four steps to the east. Keep going until your child finds the object.

Variations: If you have a compass in your car, you could have your child note the sequence of directions to a particular place.

- Your kinesthetic learner will do well because she is able to move throughout the entire activity.

- For your visual learner, you can have the directions written on a piece of paper large enough for her to read from a distance.

- Your auditory learner should repeat the directions to you as you write them down.

Mastery occurs when: your child can either move in the correct direction or tell you the correct direction in which to move to get to an object.

You may want to help your child a little more if: she can't identify the correct direction. You may want to begin the activity using only cardinal directions.

Geography

Some of the things your child will learn about in geography are the various landforms and bodies of water in the United States, including bays, bluffs, canyons, cliffs, coasts, deserts, gulfs, harbors, hills, islands, lakes, mountains, oceans, peaks, peninsulas, plains, plateaus, rivers, seas, shores, straits, swamps, valleys, and volcanoes.

Your child will need to know these landforms and be able to identify them on a map as well as in the real world. The following table describes some important skills related to landforms, where children can run into problems, and what you can do to help them along.

Geography Skills	Having Problems?	Quick Tips
Names and recognizes several landforms.	Knows only about landforms in your town.	Make some landforms: use mud or sand, draw pictures, make mountains out of molehills. Get creative!
Knows the symbols that represent landforms on a map.	Gets confused by the extra map symbols.	Make some flash cards with the landform symbol on one side and the name of the landform on the other.

Geography Activities

1 My Book of Landforms

TIME: 1–2 hours (can be divided into shorter time periods)

MATERIALS
- list of landforms (see top of this page)
- paper
- pencils
- dictionary
- colored pencils

Learning happens when: your child writes the name of one landform on each sheet of paper. Then have him look up the definition of each landform in a dictionary and write it on the appropriate page. Discuss each one with your child. Ask him to draw a picture that represents each landform and color it.

Variations: You can ask your child to make small models of each type of landform and mount them with a label and the definition on poster board.

Your child will enjoy the variation where he gets to make the models.

👁 Your visual learner will learn well from the activity and its variation.

👂 Ask your child to record his descriptions of each type of landform as if he were making a tour guide's speech.

Mastery occurs when: your child can identify each type of landform and give a short description of it.

You may want to help your child a little more if: he cannot identify the different types of landforms. You could start by focusing on a couple of landforms at a time, then adding others.

2 Landform Scavenger Hunt

Learning happens when: your child writes a landform name on each index card. Shuffle the cards, then have your child draw one card at a time. Ask her to look through the magazines and find a picture of the type of landform that she picked from the index cards. Continue with this procedure until she has found eight to twelve different landforms.

TIME: 20–30 minutes

MATERIALS
list of landforms (see page 188)
index cards
pencils
magazines

Variations: If you have more than one child or would like to play yourself, you can turn this activity into a game. Each player draws five cards. Then the race is on as each player looks through the magazines to find his or her five landforms. The one who finds his or her five landforms first is the winner. The group should go over each player's pictures to make sure they are a good representation of the landforms, then cut the pictures out and set them aside for later use.

✋ Your child will probably learn best from the race format because she is moving more.

👁 Your visual learner will like this activity either way because she will see a visual representation of the landform.

👂 Your auditory learner should be encouraged to talk throughout this activity as she is identifying the landforms or cutting out the pictures.

Mastery occurs when: your child can find examples of the landforms in the magazines.

You may want to help your child a little more if: she cannot find examples of the landforms. Do the activity with fewer cards and not in the race format, since that would put more pressure on her.

3 Landform Rap

TIME: 30–40 minutes

MATERIALS
▪ list of landforms (see page 188) and their definitions
▪ paper
▪ pencils

Learning happens when: your child makes up a song or rap with the names of the landforms and their definitions. You'll probably want to limit the number of landforms your child has in a song. Ask him to perform the song for you and your family. If your child is intimidated by writing a rap, then call it a rhyme—same thing, different name.

Variations: Group the landforms in some way.

✋ Encourage your child to make up actions to go with each verse or definition in the song.

👁 Ask your child to draw a picture to use as a visual aid for his performance.

👂 This activity is naturally appealing to your auditory learner.

Mastery occurs when: your child can identify landforms and use some of them in a song.

You may want to help your child a little more if: he is having difficulty identifying landforms. Limit the amount he uses at a time. You might want to get him started by doing a short example yourself.

4 Landform Bingo

Learning happens when: you and your child make a bingo card with the name of a landform in each space, except the middle one. The middle space should be labeled "Free Space." You should also have your child write the name of each landform and its definition on an index card. Have her put a bean on the free space. Then read the first definition. Your child should put a bean on the square with the name of the landform that goes with the definition. Get another card and repeat the procedure until your child has five in a row—bingo!

TIME: 20–30 minutes

MATERIALS
- paper divided into a 5 × 5 grid
- index cards
- pencils
- list of landforms (see page 188) and their definitions
- beans or something to mark your space

✋ Put the index cards into a container and ask your child to select the cards herself.

👁 Draw a small picture of the landform in each grid space. This way your child will be able to see a picture as well as the written word.

👂 Repeat each definition at least twice, and have your child name aloud each landform she gets.

Mastery occurs when: your child can identify the landform that goes with each definition.

You may want to help your child a little more if: she can't identify the correct landform that goes with each definition. You could modify the bingo card so that it has fewer squares and fewer landforms to identify. You may want to group the landforms in some way, such as those that have water and those that don't.

Park Brochure

TIME: 40–60 minutes

MATERIALS

■ list of landforms (see page 188) and their definitions
■ brochure
■ paper
■ markers or colored pencils

Learning happens when: your child brainstorms a nature park he wants to create. Help him think of what type of landforms should be included in the park. Look at a brochure from another place and let your child see how it is set up. Discuss with him how the brochure should be folded and what information should go in each part of it. After your child has made his decisions, help him draw a map of the nature park. Make sure he has included at least five different types of landforms. He should describe each one in the brochure. Decide on a name for the park and color the whole brochure to make it attractive.

Variations: Your child can use publishing software to create the brochure on the computer. Most publishing software has a brochure as one of the format choices. The computer version will look more professional and can also include actual photographs of the landforms.

- Ask your child to make a three-dimensional model of the park he has designed.

- Your visual learner will benefit from making the brochure either by hand or on the computer.

- Your auditory learner can produce the brochure on the computer and add audio describing his park's features. There are many types of software that will be helpful. Some computers have a feature that will translate your child's spoken words into text.

Mastery occurs when: your child can choose landforms for his park and describe them correctly in the brochure.

You may want to help your child a little more if: he cannot understand how to describe the landforms in the brochure. Try reading each landform's definition to him while he is looking at a picture of it. Ask him how he could describe this landform in the brochure without using the exact same words.

6 Topographic Map

Copy the graphic organizer below by hand or print one from www.knowledgeessentials.com.

TIME: 30–40 minutes

MATERIALS
topographic map of the United States
paper
pencils

Type of Landform	Specific Name of the Landform	Questions About the Landform
Mountain ranges		
Oceans		
Plains		
Rivers		
Islands		
Canyons		
Deserts		
Peninsulas		

Learning happens when: your child examines the topographic map. She will be able to touch and feel the differences in height and size of the various landforms in the United States. Have your child fill in the specific name of a landform and any questions she might have on the graphic organizer. A question might be: Which mountain range has the highest elevation?

Variations: You can classify the landforms into separate groups on the organizer, such as those that have water and those that don't. You can also have specific questions written on the organizer that you want your child to answer, and add a column for answering the questions.

✋ This activity is naturally appealing to your kinesthetic learner. The topographic map allows her to touch and feel the size and shape of the various landforms.

👁 This activity is also appealing to your visual learner because she can see the differences in the various landforms.

👂 Encourage your child to pretend that she is in an airplane flying over the United States. Ask her to describe the landforms she is seeing.

Mastery occurs when: your child can see and feel the differences in the size and shape of the landforms and can make up or answer questions about them.

You may want to help your child a little more if: she cannot answer your questions about the landforms. You might try limiting your questions to one type of landform at a time.

7 | Landforms in the United States

TIME: 40–60 minutes

MATERIALS
▪ map of the United States (you can find one at www .knowledgeessentials.com)
▪ list of landforms (see page 188) and their definitions
▪ PowerPoint software

Learning happens when: your child uses the map to identify the various landforms in the United States and creates a PowerPoint presentation on them. PowerPoint is slide-show software that comes with most PCs. Your child should create at least one slide for each type of landform with the name of the landform, the definition, and specific examples in the United States. It should also include a picture of the landform.

Variations: if you want to get more complicated, you can have a slide for each specific example of a landform in the United States. Allow your child to use a topographic map to identify the landforms.

 Creating the PowerPoint presentation will appeal to your kinesthetic learner because he is constantly moving in some way.

👁 This activity is appealing to your visual learner because he is getting the information from a map and creating a visual presentation to show to other people.

👂 Ask your child to give an oral presentation of the slide show to you or a small group.

Mastery occurs when: your child can present his information about landforms correctly.

You may want to help your child a little more if: he includes incorrect information or pictures on the slides. Ask questions that will guide him in choosing information.

8 | Rivers of the United States

Learning happens when: your child looks at the U.S. map and traces the Mississippi River and its tributaries with her finger. Locate other major rivers and let her trace them with her finger. Using a blue map pencil, have your child draw the rivers on the outline of the U.S. map. Make sure she labels each river with its name. You can ask your child questions about the rivers: Which river is the longest? Which river is closest to us?

Variations: You can already have the rivers drawn on the map and just have your child label them.

TIME: 30–40 minutes

MATERIALS

▪ map of the United States (you can find one at www .knowledgeessentials.com)

▪ blue map pencil

▪ map outline of the United States (you can find one at www .knowledgeessentials.com)

Your child can make a three-dimensional model of the U.S. rivers. An outline of the U.S. map can be drawn on a large piece of cardboard. Then she can use modeling clay or Play-Doh to shape the rivers onto the map.

Ask your child to find actual pictures of the rivers, make a collage of them, and label each river with its name.

Your child can say the names of the rivers as she is labeling them, then repeat them at the end of the activity.

Mastery occurs when: your child can label each river with the correct name. Eventually she should be able to label the rivers without looking at a map.

You may want to help your child a little more if: she cannot identify and label the names of the rivers. Start with just a few rivers—for example, the Mississippi River and its tributaries. Add more as your child masters the previous group.

Economics

I want this! I want that! My friend has one of those and I need one, too. Your child is a consumer; isn't it great? It's time for your third grader to learn how much things cost and what it takes to earn that money. The first part of learning how much things cost and what it takes to earn that money is learning the basics of *supply* and *demand*. These are really two separate things, but they are almost always talked about together.

Supply is how much of something is available. For example, if you have nine candy bars, then your *supply* of candy bars is nine.

Demand is how much of something people want. It sounds a bit harder to measure, but it really isn't. To measure *demand*, we can use a very simple numbering system, just like the one used to calculate *supply*. If eight people want candy bars, then we say that the *demand* for candy bars is eight.

The following table describes some skills related to economics, where children can run into problems, and what you can do to help them along.

Economics Skills	Having Problems?	Quick Tips
Has a realistic concept of money.	Has no concept of the value of a dollar.	You can help your child with this concept by assigning her chores with a dollar value tied to part of her allowance. For example, how many times would your child have to take out the trash to be able to buy a toy or go to a movie?
Understands that there is a finite supply of goods and services.	Is convinced that there is always *more* of something.	The perfect time to talk about finite supply is when you are getting gas for your car (or buying home heating oil, or another petroleum-based product). Why is gasoline so expensive? Talk about how the limited supply of fossil fuels makes the cost of them continue to increase.
Understands that the number of people that want a good or service is called the demand for that good or service.	Doesn't understand that the more people that want something means there is a high demand for it.	As you talk with your child about supply at the gas pumps, talk about demand. Why does the price of gas keep going up? This occurs not only because of the limited supply of gas, but also because so many people want to use it.

Economics Activities

1 Supply and Demand

Learning happens when: you offer your child a candy bar for $1. More than likely, he will agree to buy it. Ask your child if he would be willing to buy it for $100. Of course, the answer would be no.

TIME: 20–30 minutes

MATERIALS
- candy bar

Your child knows $100 is way too much for a candy bar. But tell him to pretend this is the very last candy bar in the world. How much would it be worth then? Hopefully he will answer that the price would increase—probably to more than the $100 you originally asked for. This is the law of supply and demand. If there is a lot of an item, the price is low; if the item is rare, the price increases.

Variations: You can get some actual items to illustrate the idea. You can also relate the idea to other resources we use in the world today, such as gas or oil.

- ✋ Your child will learn best by actually manipulating the objects or by using pretend money to buy the items from you.

- 👁 Your visual learner will learn best from having the actual items in front of him or at least a picture of the items.

- 👂 Your child can produce a radio advertisement for both situations, including having a lot of one item or being lucky enough to have the only one in the world for sale.

Mastery occurs when: your child can demonstrate an understanding of the law of supply and demand and how it relates to the price of an item.

You may want to help your child a little more if: he does not understand that if there is only one of the item, the price will go up; if there is a lot of the item, the price will go down. Continue to find real-world examples to share with your child.

2 Piggy Bank

Learning happens when: your child identifies something that she really wants to buy. Go to the store to see how much the item costs. Sit down with your child to discuss how she can earn the money to buy the object. Make a plan of what she decides. It might be washing the dishes, weeding the garden, or anything else that she is capable of doing. Decide how much money she can earn by performing various jobs. Your child can then start earning money and saving it in her piggy bank to buy the object. When she has earned enough money, take her to the store and let her buy the object.

Variations: It would be a good idea for your child to keep track of how long it takes her to earn the money. She could keep a daily, weekly, or monthly record depending on the cost of the object and how long it takes to save for it.

- ✋ Your kinesthetic learner will probably enjoy doing any kind of job that requires movement and will certainly enjoy counting the money.

- 👁 Have your visual child make a graph of the time spent working and the amount of money she earns each week.

- 👂 Your child can keep a graph and can periodically verbalize how much money she has earned so far and how much money she still needs.

Mastery occurs when: your child can understand that things she wants cost money, and it takes hard work to earn the money.

You may want to help your child a little more if: she cannot understand the concept of earning money for the things she wants. Start with items that she could earn in a week or two, then build up to larger items that cost more money.

TIME: Varies

MATERIALS
- piggy bank or something to keep money in
- object your child wants to buy

3 | How Much Is That?

TIME: 40–60 minutes

MATERIALS

list of common items to buy

paper

pencils

Make a chart like the one below of things that you buy often.

Shopping Items	Prediction of Costs	Actual Cost
Pizza		
Shoes		
Music CD		
Shirt		
Shorts		
Video game		
Ice cream		

Learning happens when: you and your child make a shopping list of things you want to buy. After the two of you have made the shopping list, ask your child how much money he thinks each item costs. Record the predictions on the chart. Go to the stores, or look in a catalog or on the Internet, to find the actual cost of each item and record it on the chart. Discuss the results with your child. You'll probably discover that he doesn't have any idea how much things actually cost.

Variations: Do the activity several times, but break the items into different categories each time, such as food, clothes, and toys.

Your kinesthetic child will like going to the store to find the price of the items.

Your visual child will like going to the store or looking in a catalog to find the prices. You can also have your child find the difference in the predicted cost and the actual cost and produce a graph to show the results.

🦻 Ask your child to repeat the predicted cost and the actual cost of the items as he records them.

Mastery occurs when: your child has a better understanding of what things really cost.

You may want to help your child a little more if: he doesn't begin to understand the cost of the items. Try making the items things he uses every day, then figure out how much these items cost over the course of one week.

4 Out on Your Own

Learning happens when: you give your child pretend money to totally support herself for a month. Decide on an amount to give her. Brainstorm everything that she will have to spend money on for a month. Put those items on a chart and work out approximately how much each item will cost for a month. The chart on page 202 is an example. Help your child find the costs by looking in newspapers, on the Internet, at some actual utility bills, and in other real-life places such as the grocery store.

After you and your child have finished the chart, add up the entire cost for the month and compare it to the amount of money available to her. Discuss the results. Note that she may have to give up some luxuries, such as new tennis shoes or a trip to the movies, in order to pay for the basics.

Variations: You can have your child pretend that she is renting a room in your house and charge her for rent and other expenses. Give her fake money and have her actually give you the money for each item.

TIME: Varies

MATERIALS
- pretend money
- paper
- pencils
- newspaper

Expense	Monthly Cost
Rent or mortgage	
Automobile payment or maintenance	
Helath insurance	
Car insurance	
Electricity	
Water	
Food	
Heat (oil or natural gas)	
Gas (for car)	
Telephone	
Clothing	
Entertainment	
Cable TV	
Internet connection	
Doctor	

✋ Your kinesthetic learner will like using fake money to pay you for each item or bill.

👁 Your visual learner will enjoy using fake money because she will be able to see her money disappear as she pays the bills. It might also be a good idea to graph the expenses in a circle graph so that she can see how much she spends on each item per month.

👂 Ask your child to use the chart or a graph of the expenses to record them on an audiotape or CD.

Mastery occurs when: your child understands that the cost of living can be very high.

You may want to help your child a little more if: she doesn't understand that the cost of living can be high. Make sure the items you brainstormed are everything she is used to having.

5 | Tracking Expenses

Learning happens when: your child keeps track of everything he buys or you buy for him in one week. Have him record the date in the notebook, then list each item and its price as he buys things or you buy things for him. List all the items purchased in one day. At the end of the day, help your child add up the total cost of purchases. Make a separate entry for each day of the week. At the end of the week, help him add up the total cost for the week. He might be surprised.

TIME: 15 minutes each day for 1 week

MATERIALS
- spiral notebook
- pencils

Variations: You can have your child separate the items into categories such as food, clothing, and entertainment.

- This activity will appeal to your kinesthetic learner because he is moving around and recording all of his expenses.

- Ask your child to make a graph of the information based on the days of the week and the total cost for each day. The graph can be divided into the categories already mentioned.

- Ask your child to make an oral presentation of the information to you or a small group.

Mastery occurs when: your child is able to understand how much money he spends on himself each month. He should be able to see the information and make conclusions from the data. For example, he might discover that he spends the most money on Saturday. He might also discover that most of the money is spent on food.

You may want to help your child a little more if: he is not able to draw conclusions from the data. Make a bar graph of the information with your child and give him an example of making a conclusion about the data.

Environmental Learning

There are many ways to incorporate map skills, geography, and economics into daily life. Go for a drive. What better way to learn about landforms than actually seeing them? If you can, take a vacation and show your child as many types of landforms as you can. Buy her a camera to take pictures of the landforms for later use.

The opportunities to talk about basic economic concepts with your child are apparent every time you go to the store, watch a TV commercial, or ask your child to do a chore. Good money sense starts at home, so demonstrate saving and wise spending every chance you get.

End of Third Grade Social Studies Checklist

Students who are working at the standard level at the end of third grade:

_____ Can create symbols for real-life objects

_____ Can identify cardinal directions on a map

_____ Can identify intermediate directions on a map

_____ Can identify the equator and prime meridian

_____ Can identify the four hemispheres of the earth

_____ Can identify basic landforms

_____ Understand the law of supply and demand

_____ Can set a financial goal and make a plan to accomplish the goal

---

Teaching Your Third Grader Thinking Skills

10

Teaching your third grader to think sounds like a lofty goal, doesn't it? You can help foster a thinking mind in your child by treating him or her as an active participant in a home where you explore "why" and "how" questions. The more opportunities your child has to explore ideas and be heard at home, the more likely he or she is to be an active thinker both in and out of school.

Teaching children to think reasonably and logically improves children's impulsive behavior and social adjustment. Children taught this way are less likely to develop behavioral difficulties than are well-adjusted children who do not learn these skills. Of course, the way you respond to your child and act in front of him or her makes the largest impact on how your child learns to think and communicate.

In a study of children from kindergarten through fourth grade (Shure, 1993) that was the culmination of twenty years of research to test

Beginning of Third Grade Thinking Skills Checklist

Students who are working at the standard level at the beginning of third grade:

_____ Start to use symbolic reasoning to complement more concrete manipulations

_____ Draw inferences

_____ Differentiate between fact and opinion

_____ Try to find answers to self-generated questions

_____ Draw conclusions

ideas about thinking skills, parent modeling, and behavior, M. B. Shure delineated four levels of communication that we use all the time:

LEVEL 1: POWER ASSERTION (DEMANDS, BELITTLES, PUNISHES)

- Do it because I say so!
- Do you want a time out?
- How many times have I told you . . . !
- If you can't share the truck, I'll take it away so that neither of you will have it.

LEVEL 2: POSITIVE ALTERNATIVE (NO EXPLANATION)

- I'm on the phone now. Go watch TV.
- Ask him for the truck.
- You should share your toys.

LEVEL 3: INDUCTION (EXPLANATIONS AND REASONS)

- I feel angry when you interrupt me.
- If you hit, you'll lose a friend (hurt him).
- You'll make him angry if you hit him (grab toys).
- You shouldn't hit (grab). It's not nice.

LEVEL 4: PROBLEM-SOLVING PROCESS (TEACHING THINKING)

- What's the problem? What's the matter?
- How do you think I (she/he) feel(s) when you hit (grab)?
- What happened (might happen) when you did (do) that?
- Can you think of a different way to solve this problem (tell him/her/me how you feel)?
- Do you think that is or is not a good idea? Why (why not)?

The parents who communicated as often as possible on level 4 in Shure's study had children who were the least impulsive, the least withdrawn, and showed the fewest behavior problems as observed by independent raters.

We all know that there are times when communicating on level 1 is the only way to go, so don't beat yourself up. You can't reason a child out of the street when a car is coming. Awareness of the communication levels enables you to implement the highest level as much of the time as possible, which in turn fosters a thinking child.

Teaching and modeling thinking encourages children to ask questions about information and ideas. It helps your child learn how to identify unstated assumptions, form and defend opinions, and see relationships between events and ideas. A thinking person raises a thinking child. That you are even reading this book assures you are a thinking person, so you are on the right track.

Don't expect your child's third grade teacher to stand up in front of the class and say "Okay, it's time to learn to think." Instead, your child's teacher will incorporate activities and language that foster the development and refinement of thinking skills, such as problem solving, concentration, and reasoning, throughout your child's daily activities. In the same way, you will foster thinking skills if you do many of the activities in this book with your child.

There are many approaches to teaching thinking. You can teach your child to use a set of identifiable skills, such as deciding between relevant and irrelevant information and generating questions from written material. This is particularly useful for auditory and visual learners. Your kinesthetic child learns to think more actively by participating in sports, hands-on projects, and similar activities.

Problem Solving

Problem solving is a hallmark of mathematical activity and a major means of developing mathematical knowledge. It is finding a way to reach a goal that is not immediately attainable. Problem solving is natural to young children because the world is new to them, and they exhibit curiosity, intelligence, and flexibility as they face new situations. The challenge at this level is to build on children's innate problem-solving inclinations and to preserve and encourage a disposition that values problem solving. Try the problem-solving math section in chapter 7 and the science activities about systems in chapter 8 as challenging opportunities for your child.

Concentration

Thinking skills begin with the ability to maintain a focus on one thing long enough to think it through. Thinking something through means understanding the information (in whatever form—for example, visual, print, or oral), questioning the information, and thinking about the alternatives before making a decision.

Concentration skills are a big part of learning to read. Your child's teacher will be working hard with him or her on concentration skills, and you can help reinforce these skills by trying the activities in the reading comprehension section of chapter 5.

Comprehension

This is a hard one. To think about something in a reasonable, logical manner, you need to understand it, but creative thinking is born from instances where you don't understand something. The trick is probably in the mix. Let your child explore new information and form creative thoughts about it, then talk to him or her logically about it. Giving your child time to think freely about new information allows him or her to think about it in many contexts and many forms before being told which concept or form is proper.

In order to better develop your child's understanding of different concepts, his or her perception should be shaped by touching, hearing, and seeing something simultaneously, to experience the concept as best as he or she can. Take time to let your child talk about what he or she is seeing, touching, and hearing. By experiencing new concepts in different contexts, your child can become aware of different aspects of an idea and develop his or her understanding of its meaning.

Reasoning

There is more than one type of reasoning. Formal reasoning skills, such as deductive and inductive reasoning, are developed at a later age. The reasoning skill that is focused on in third grade is spatial-temporal reasoning, or the ability to visualize and transform objects in space.

Spatial-temporal operations are responsible for combining separate elements of an object into a single whole, or for arranging objects in a specific spatial order. Spatial-temporal operations require successive steps; each step is dependent on previous ones.

Spatial-temporal skills are the most frequently tested reasoning/thinking skills on IQ and other standardized tests. You can work on these skills with your child through the math and science activities in this book.

Logic

Children learn about and understand logical concepts in different ways. In math, for example, some kids think about numbers in terms of where they are on a number line, while other kids think about how many objects make up each number. These children reach an understanding of numbers, their meaning, and how to use them, but they reach it in different ways. Taking this example further, these children comprehend the information and understand what numbers represent. But if one group is then asked to handle the numbers in different contexts, the group will need to be aware of different aspects of numbers in order to develop a fuller understanding of their meaning. The group can then think about numbers in different ways and apply them to different situations in a logical way rather than simply recall what they mean.

A large part of logical thinking stems from the ability to see objects and apply concepts in many contexts (spatial-temporal reasoning applies here). Teaching children to question information teaches them to think about the information in more than one context before making a logical conclusion about it. Logical thinking can be reinforced during the discipline process by applying logical consequences to a behavior rather than using an arbitrary punishment.

Thinking Skills Activities

To help your child develop thinking skills, you can:

- Encourage her to ask questions about the world around her.
- Ask him to imagine what will happen next in the story when you are reading together.
- Actively listen to your child's conversation, responding seriously and nonjudgmentally to her questions.
- Ask what he is feeling and why when he expresses feelings.
- Suggest that she find facts to support her opinions, and encourage her to locate information relevant to her opinions.
- Use entertainment—a book, a TV program, or a movie—as the basis of family discussions.
- Use daily activities as occasions for learning (environmental learning).
- Reward him for inquisitive and/or creative activity that is productive.
- Ask her what she learned at school.

Environmental Learning

There are thousands of ways that you can use your child's everyday environment to encourage thinking skills. Remember, if your child is an active participant in a home where there are "why" and "how" discussions, he or she is more likely to be an active thinker both in and out of school.

End of Third Grade Thinking Skills Checklist

Students who are working at the standard level at the end of third grade:

_____ Use symbolic reasoning to complement more concrete manipulations

_____ Draw inferences

_____ Seek answers to self-generated questions

_____ Draw conclusions based on fact and opinion

_____ Know and begin to use thinking processes, such as the scientific process and the writer's process

---

Assessment

11

A key component to learning is evaluating what has been learned. Assessment serves several different purposes:

1. Assessing individual student abilities and knowledge and adapting instructions accordingly

2. Evaluating and improving the instructional program in general

3. Determining individual student eligibility for promotion or graduation, college admission, or special honors

4. Measuring and comparing school, school district, statewide, and national performance for broad public accountability

There is more than one kind of assessment and more than one context in which this term is frequently used. There are multiple ways that you and your child's teacher assess your child. There is broad assessment of your child's knowledge of certain things and his performance as compared to other children of the same age and grade. Standardized assessment is usually done at the end of the year and comprises many sessions of test taking in a short time period. There are uses for all types of assessment.

Assessing Individual Student Abilities and Knowledge

Students learn in different ways, so teachers assess their daily learning in different ways. The most common way to assess daily learning is by observing how your child responds to and implements things that he or she learns in the classroom. As teachers observe and consider the variety of daily assignments of students, they begin to help their students demonstrate this learning on tests.

Observation and Portfolio Assessment

Your child's overall progress is assessed by considering her developmental stage and cognitive learning abilities with key concepts and key skills within the framework of her learning styles. Teachers (and by now, you) do this by observing your child on a daily basis, giving basic skills tests, gauging reaction and comprehension time when given new information, and asking frequent, informal questions. All of the activities in this book include explanations for how to assess your child's performance, and the checklists at the beginning and end of the chapters can help you assess your child's progress in each skill.

Teachers have begun to implement portfolio assessment more frequently. Teachers are giving your child the opportunity to demonstrate learning through a variety of activities, such as art projects, writing activities, oral presentations, and daily participation with unit tests, to determine the true levels of comprehension and skill development with the variety of materials and skills in each learning unit. Many people think portfolio assessment is one of the most accurate methods of determining learning, but it can be subjective, so it has been criticized. Teachers try really hard not to be subjective; contrary to what some people think, they aren't likely to retaliate for a mishap with a parent by lowering the child's grades. When a child succeeds, the teacher has also succeeded. Discounting the child's success because of personal feelings destroys the teacher's professional success.

Always remember (even if your child does really well) that achievement tests are just one measure of your child's learning. You know this is true because you have been using rough measures in the activities you do with your child. Observation is a primary assessment tool.

Standardized Testing

Testing is a hot topic, and rightly so. We all remember the standardized tests—spending days filling in little circles with a number 2 pencil.

The majority of teachers dislike standardized testing for a number of reasons. Sure, there is the issue of accountability. But the heart of the issue is not that teachers are afraid of being held to a standard to keep their job—it is that they disagree with being held to what many of them believe is a false standard. Think about how an auditory or physical learner will do on a test designed for visual learners. The tests aren't an accurate picture of what all learners can do.

In defense of test makers, they are doing their best to adjust their approaches within the limitations of state requirements, logistical requirements, and traditional business practices. But the system within which teachers, parents, students, and test makers are trying to operate is definitely imperfect.

Others' issues are centered around "teaching the test." Teachers are afraid the curriculum they are told to teach will be so narrowly geared toward the test that it will limit their ability to teach the things that support the tested items. They are concerned they will only be able to teach to the cognitive learning level when they know the student should also be able to apply the knowledge, synthesize it, and evaluate it. We have discussed how individual scores can be invalid, but so can group scores. Test results may be invalidated by teaching so narrowly to the objectives of a particular test that scores are raised without actually improving the broader, often more important, set of academic skills that the test should be measuring.

At the end of the day, assessment is a very strong tool. It encourages, discourages, and measures learning. Assessment should be a means of fostering growth toward high expectations and should support student learning. When assessments are used in thoughtful and meaningful ways and combined with information from other sources, students' scores provide important information that can lead to decisions that promote student learning and equality of opportunity. The misuse of tests for high-stakes purposes (tests that are used to make significant educational decisions about children, teachers, schools, or school districts) has undermined the benefits these tests can foster.

The standardized tests that cause so much controversy are norm-referenced tests, meaning the test questions are selected so that a national sample of students' test scores will result in a normal distribution: there will always be a group of students at the bottom, a majority in the middle, and a group at the top. It is unrealistic to expect whole groups of students to be in the top percentiles (or groups) on these tests. Most students are expected to perform near the fiftieth percentile.

Helping Your Child Test Well

You play a vital role in helping your child succeed on standardized tests. Here are just a few things you can do:

- Put your child at ease by discussing your own experiences with taking tests. If you were nervous or anxious, talk about it. Let him know those feelings are normal.

- Be aware of the specific days tests will be given. Ask your child how the testing sessions are going. Offer encouragement.

- Stress the importance of listening to test directions and following them carefully. Provide practice activities at home, such as following a recipe or reading and answering questions about a story.

- Make sure your child goes to bed early every night and at the same time every night, especially on the night before testing.

- Encourage healthy eating, rest, and exercise.

- Most standardized testing is given over a three- or four-day period. Ask your child's teacher for a schedule, and make sure your child attends school on those days.

- Meet with your child's teachers to discuss the results. If your child had difficulty in specific areas, ask teachers for suggestions in the form of homework assignments, techniques, and specific material.

What the Scores Really Mean

High-stakes tests are used to make significant educational decisions about children, teachers, schools, or school districts. To use a single objective test in the determination of such things as graduation, course credit, grade placement, promotion to the next grade, or placement in special groups is a serious misuse of tests. Remember, your child's score on a standardized test is only one measure of what he knows. Most schools use multiple measures, including student projects, homework, portfolios, chapter tests, and oral reports.

Measuring and Comparing School, School District, Statewide, and National Performance for Broad Public Accountability

Increasingly, policy makers at the federal, state, and local levels want to identify ways to measure student performance in order to see how well the public education system is doing its job. The goals of this accountability approach include providing information about the status of the educational system, motivating desired change, measuring program effectiveness, and creating systems for rewarding and sanctioning educators based on the performance of their students.

The use of testing to change classroom instruction is central to the theory of standards-based reform. It assumes that educators and the public can agree on what should be taught; that a set of clear standards can be developed, which in turn drive curriculum and instruction; and that tests can measure how well students perform based on those standards.

Third Grade Society　　12

Your third grader lives in a microcosm of your world—there are no bills to pay, but there are definitely social considerations that are taking on a life of their own. In this chapter, we'll take a look at the third grade social scene and how it may be affecting your child's school experience.

Birthday Parties

Birthday parties are a *big* occasion for third graders. It is very exciting to receive mail or a note, and an invitation is even better. An upcoming birthday party is the talk of the playground. It is exciting for the birthday boy or girl, because he or she is the center of attention, and it feels good knowing people want to go to the party. It is exciting for those who are invited, because birthday parties are so much fun. But it can be excruciating for those who are not invited. Even if your child is always invited to every party given by his friends, you should make sure he understands that other children may not be invited and it may hurt their feelings if he talks about the party in front of them.

If the kids your child considers to be his friends exclude him from a party, this is going to be hard for you and your child. Maybe the other child's parents limited the number of children that could be invited. Maybe your child accidentally did something to hurt his friend's feelings. Maybe the birthday girl isn't as good of a friend as your child perceives her to be. No matter what the case is, your child is probably feeling hurt and you are the best person to help him right now. Try planning something that the two of you can do together during the time of the party. Your child feels like he is not special when something like this happens, so try to lift his spirits by making him feel special.

If you're the one giving the party, the general etiquette is to only send invitations to school if the entire class is invited. Otherwise, invitations should be distributed outside school. This will not stop the chatter on the playground, but at least those who were not invited will not have their noses rubbed in it, as invitations are given to a select few.

It is important that your child be gracious about all of the gifts that he receives. Sit down with him and write a thank-you note that he can use as a guide for writing the others. Help him find something nice to say about each gift.

Catch Me If You Can

Developmentally, third graders mostly play with friends of the same sex (see chapter 2). However, they are starting to develop an interest in members of the opposite sex. It is not as strong as a crush, but more of a curiosity. This can get interesting on the playground. Sometimes there will be brief conversations between interested parties, but that approach is uncommonly sophisticated at this age. Instead, to show interest, they chase each other, tease each other, and generally try to annoy each another. The bigger the reaction, the better for the chaser/teaser/annoyer. Most of the time it is innocent fun; sometimes it can get out of hand, however, especially if the interest is in the form of teasing a more sensitive third grader.

If your third grader is experiencing some of this behavior, talk to her about it. Sometimes a simple explanation that the person likes your child and does not know how to show it will be sufficient. If, however, your child is upset by the behavior and talking about it does not help, you may need to talk to the teacher about it. If your child is the one who is chasing or teasing, you may suggest other ways to act, such as talking to the person, asking the person to play, and so on.

Bullies

A major issue in most schools is dealing with bullies. Unfortunately, bullying starts as early as kindergarten. In third grade, bullying can take the form of name-calling, exclusion, teasing, and less frequently, physical intimidation. Schools are acutely aware of the problem, and many have programs to prevent it.

Bullies behave in inappropriate ways because they can get away with it and they do not have the skills to interact appropriately. Bullies are a sad bunch. They boast, brag, and display false confidence, but they often feel inadequate inside, and they use inappropriate means to get power and attention. Bullies often get other kids to join in. It is shocking to see some of the nicest kids joining with the bully. Often, however, those collaborating with the bully in his activities are just glad he is concentrating on someone else.

If your child is being bullied, it can be difficult to know how to best help him. Sometimes ignoring the bully will stop the behavior. Bullies love the reaction, and if there isn't one, some bullies will get bored and move on. Standing up to a bully might stop the behavior. Bullies rely on intimidation. If their target is not intimidated, they will go on to the next victim. If standing up to a bully does not work, you may need to talk to the teacher.

Bullies pick their targets carefully. They pick those whom they perceive will be easy to tease, pick on, or intimidate. This is absolutely not to blame the victim, but if your child is being bullied, the bully perceives some weakness. You may want to consider getting your child involved in an activity that will boost his self-confidence. Tae kwon do or another sport can be a confidence booster. The purpose of these physical activities is not to turn your child into a fighter; rather, it is to build his self-esteem. Bullies will perceive your child as confident and will probably leave him alone.

If your child is the bully, you need to take action. Ask yourself some tough questions: Is your child doing this to get attention that he feels is lacking at home? Are you a bully? Remember that you must—absolutely must—act in front or your child how you want him to act.

If your child's behavior is truly a mystery, then get him involved in activities to build his confidence and encourage teamwork. Team sports would be a great outlet. You can also work closely with the school. Talk to your child's teacher about your concerns. Ask what behaviors your child exhibits at school. Teachers are concerned with bullying and would be very happy to work with you to help change your child's behavior. Make a list with your child's teacher of one to five of the most troubling behaviors. Have the teacher make a checklist and mark whether your child exhibits these behaviors daily. You will receive this sheet every day, sign it, and have your child take the sheet back to the teacher.

Have some rewards for your child if he has a good day or a good week. They do not have to be expensive material rewards. Your child would love to have some of your undivided attention. So one reward may be to spend a half hour together playing a game or going to the park. By focusing on your child, you are sending a message that he is important, and that will make his spirits soar.

That's Not Fair!

Ah, the plaintive cry of third graders everywhere. You probably hear it at home. Teachers hear it at school. Third graders have a strong sense of justice, and they will rail against the perceived injustice they see everywhere. Third graders are acutely aware of what is going on with other people, especially fellow classmates and siblings. If they feel their classmates or siblings have received some sort of favor that they have not received, they will cry foul.

One concept third graders have difficulty with is that fair does not necessarily mean the same treatment for everyone. A high school–age sibling probably has a different bedtime than a third grader. A biting two-year-old would be punished differently from a biting third grader. A child with learning disabilities may have a shorter assignment than the other third graders. Usually, just talking to your third grader will make the situation seem a little less unfair.

Extracurricular Activities

There are numerous opportunities for third graders to be involved in all kinds of classes and sports outside of school. Parents want their children to have all the opportunities they did not have as children. This can lead to overscheduling.

There are reasons children need unscheduled free time. Your child needs time to play with her friends. Unstructured play with friends teaches social skills, such as cooperation, compromise, taking turns, leadership, and how to resolve differences peacefully (and on one's own). Unscheduled free time allows your child to use her imagination, to be creative, and to explore things. A child whose time is scheduled down to the minute misses out on many positives.

That being said, sports and classes can be invaluable to your child. Playing sports gives her the opportunity to learn specialized skills while also learning teamwork, cooperation, and how to win and lose gracefully. Sports get your child out and exercising, which is very important. Classes can give your child the opportunity to learn something new.

Your child is growing up fast. Third grade is a special year. Friendships become more important, and the bond between best friends deepens. Your child will want to extend those friendships outside the school. She will benefit from well-chosen extracurricular activities balanced with unscheduled free time to play and explore. While outside relationships are becoming more important, you are still the most significant person in your child's life. She wants to spend time with you. Spending uninterrupted free time with your child will make her feel very loved and important.

Moving On to Fourth Grade

You made it! Your third grader is now going to be a fourth grader, and you are going to be the parent of a fourth grader!

You can monitor your child's readiness for fourth grade and determine areas that need reinforcement with the following subject area and developmental checklists.

Ready to Go

Students who are ready to go on to fourth grade:

Reading

_____ Read with understanding and fluency

_____ Understand the meaning of synonyms, antonyms, and homonyms

_____ Identify the meanings of compound words

_____ Use punctuation cues to add meaning to the text

_____ Use graphic organizers to aid comprehension

_____ Make reasonable predictions

_____ Identify the main idea of a passage

_____ Identify character traits

_____ Summarize what has been read

_____ Have a larger sight vocabulary

Writing

_____ Communicate in writing

_____ Use writing to inform others

_____ Use writing to persuade others

_____ Identify nouns, verbs, adjectives, and adverbs in a sentence

_____ Use adjectives to describe things and enhance their writing

_____ Correctly use conjunctions

_____ Correctly use common spelling rules

_____ Identify sentence types

_____ Write compound sentences

Math

_____ Comfortably add or subtract large numbers

_____ Know the basic multiplication and division facts

_____ Understand how place value works in our number system

_____ Are able to round numbers in order to make a reasonable estimate

_____ Are able to use tools such as rulers to measure the area and perimeter of squares and rectangles and thermometers to measure temperature

_____ Differentiate solids from shapes

_____ Find fractions of a whole and fractions of a set

_____ Understand how bar graphs, line graphs, and tables communicate information in math

Science

_____ Observe, record, and communicate changes

_____ Measure length in centimeters, mass in grams, and temperature in degrees Celsius

_____ Classify objects and organisms

_____ Know about systems and subsystems

_____ Tell how sound is produced and travels

_____ Understand the characteristics, basic needs, and habitats of organisms

_____ Know how organisms fit together in a food chain

_____ Understand that forces such as earthquakes, glaciers, volcanoes, and erosion change the earth

Anxieties

There are always going to be anxieties when moving on to another grade. After all, you just got to know the third grade teacher and you really like her. And who will be the homeroom mom next year? Wait—this is supposed to be about the children's anxieties, right? Wrong. Everyone is going to feel a little sad, a little anxious, a little excited, and really glad it is summer when the subject of fourth grade arises.

Minimizing "Brain Drain"

Now that your child has acquired tangible skills that are building blocks for future learning, you are facing your fourth year of the challenge of keeping those skills fresh. Here are some things to keep in mind to help your child retain his or her third grade skills during the summer months.

Do

• Reinforce skills from his or her third grade year through environmental learning.

- Go to the library on a regular basis.
- Include learning activities in your weekly summer routine.
- Encourage free and creative thinking through art projects or active play.

DON'T

- Try to "get ahead" for the next year.
- Have your child spend the whole summer with a tutor.
- Ignore obvious learning opportunities (such as mapping out the trip to Grandma's).

Your child's third grade year has been enhanced, supported, and furthered by your efforts. Continue creating the learning environment that you worked so hard on this year over the summer and into fourth grade. You are on the right track.

LITERATURE FOR THIRD GRADERS

This section contains a list of books that your child may find interesting and lists learning activities along with the reading selections. You can find more recommended literature for your third grader at www.knowledgeessentials.com.

Night of the Twisters

Author: Ivy Ruckman

Publisher: HarperCollins Publishers

A series of tornadoes hits a community in Nebraska. Dan and his best friend are home alone when the storm hits and take shelter in the basement. The house is destroyed. The tornadoes hit the community again and again. Family members are separated with no means of communication.

Special Considerations: Your child should be able to read this book on her own. You might have to help with some of the weather vocabulary words.

Learning: Learn the facts about tornadoes. How are they classified? In which states do tornadoes occur the most often? What should you do if you are caught outdoors when a tornado hits? If you are in a state where tornadoes occur, make a family emergency plan.

Activity: Use the Internet or a resource book to find data on the number of tornadoes that occurred in each state during a particular year.

Make a graph or a chart to display the information. This could be done on poster board or with a computer program.

Follow-Up: When the graph or chart is completed, ask your child questions about it.

Why Mosquitoes Buzz in People's Ears

Author: Verna Aardema
Publisher: Puffin Books

An African myth explains why mosquitoes buzz in people's ears. A mosquito causes a series of events among the animals that leads to the killing of a baby owl. The mother owl is so upset that she doesn't do her duty of waking the sun. When the other animals figure out what happened, they blame the mosquito and are angry with him. The reason the mosquito buzzes in people's ears is to ask if they are still angry with him.

Special Considerations: This is a short picture book that your child might think is too easy for him. Encourage your child to read it and identify the reason the mosquito buzzes in people's ears so that he can create his own myth.

Learning: Explain what a myth is. Discuss the various African animals.

Activity: Have your child write his own myth explaining a natural phenomenon.

Follow-Up: Read other myths either from the African culture or some other culture. Discuss the similarities and differences with your child.

Abe's Island

Author: William Steig
Publisher: Farrar, Straus and Giroux

A well-to-do mouse named Abe is on a picnic with his wife, Amanda. A storm comes and they hide out in a cave. Amanda's scarf blows off.

When Abe tries to save it, he is blown away and ends up at the top of a tree on an island. Abe is forced to try to survive on this island. He finds there are many things he can do. He meets many interesting creatures as he tries out many escape plans to get off the island and back to his family.

Special Considerations: You might want to read this book with your child so that you can discuss the vocabulary words with him.

Learning: Discuss basic needs and survival skills with your child. What would you have done if you had been stranded on this island? How did the character change from the beginning of the story to the end?

Activity: As you are reading, have your child keep track of the ways that Abe tries to escape the island. Try keeping the information in a chart. When you have finished the story, have your child make a book of his own illustrations of Abe's attempts to escape.

Follow-Up: Talk about how the story would be different if the characters were humans instead of animals.

Charlotte's Web
Author: E. B. White
Publisher: HarperTrophy

A spider named Charlotte becomes friends with a pig named Wilbur. Wilbur is supposed to be slaughtered at Christmas, but Charlotte helps save his life. The book explores the friendships of the animals on the farm.

Special Considerations: Your child should be able to read this book on her own. She might need some help with the meanings of some of the words. This would be a good book to have your child practice using context clues to figure out the meaning. After she has read a chapter, have her retell the story to you.

Learning: This is a great book to teach about friendship. What would you be willing to do for your friend? What has a friend done for you?

Activity: Have your child make a list of the characteristics that she would want a good friend to have. Discuss why she would want these characteristics in her friends. Ask her which of these characteristics she possesses. Which ones does she need to practice?

Follow-Up: Have your child rank the characteristics from most important to least important.

Amber Brown Is Not a Crayon

Author: Paula Danziger
Publisher: Putnam

Amber and Justin are best friends. They do everything together. One day they learn that Justin has to move to Alabama.

Special Considerations: Your child should be able to read this book on his own.

Learning: Use this book to discuss feelings. Amber has to deal with being teased about her name and also with her feelings about Justin moving away. Ask your child these questions: Have you ever been teased by someone? How did it make you feel? Has someone you were close to ever moved away? How did that make you feel?

Activity: Brainstorm with your child what you could do to make someone feel better. Choose an action and have your child draw a picture of someone doing that.

Follow-Up: Have your child choose one of the ideas to make someone feel better and practice by doing it every day for a week. Discuss how it felt to make someone else feel better. How did it make your child feel?

Tales of a Fourth Grade Nothing

Author: Judy Blume
Publisher: Dutton Children's Books

Peter Hatcher feels like a nothing thanks to his little brother Fudge. Fudge is into everything, so he receives most of his parents' attention.

Fudge is always causing some sort of problem for Peter. He even swallows Peter's pet turtle, Dribble.

Special Considerations: Your child should be able to read this book on her own.

Learning: This book would be a good way to explore how to deal with a younger sibling. Would you have done the same things Peter did or something different?

Activity: Have your child make a list of the problems Fudge caused Peter. Which ones did you enjoy reading about the most? Do you think all of these things could really happen?

Follow-Up: Have your child brainstorm some ways that a person could deal with the problems caused by a younger sibling.

Freckle Juice

Author: Judy Blume

Publisher: Simon & Schuster

Andrew is fascinated by freckles. He wants them so badly that he pays Sheila fifty cents for the secret of a drink to make freckles. Andrew learns a lesson at the end that not everything works the way someone tells you it does.

Special Considerations: Your child should be able to read this book on his own. Just beware if he starts mixing the ingredients to the secret recipe.

Learning: Your child will learn that some people will tell you what you want to hear to cheat you out of money or to make fun of you. It is also a good reminder to be happy with yourself just the way you are.

Activity: Research what types of people generally have freckles. How many people in your child's class have freckles? Get some data and make a chart or graph with the information.

Follow-Up: What really causes people to have freckles? Research this with your child to find out the answer.

Sarah Plain and Tall
Author: Patricia MacLachlan
Publisher: HarperTrophy

A woman named Sarah answers the advertisement of a widower with two children who is looking for a wife. Sarah misses her home in Maine but falls in love with the children. The children are afraid she will leave them one day just as their mother left them.

Special Considerations: Because of the theme of family and the feelings of abandonment, it might be best to read this book with your child.

Learning: What makes a family? Use this book to teach about blended families. Also discuss the feelings of children who have lost a parent.

Activity: Have your child brainstorm what makes a family. Have your child draw a picture of her family and write what makes each person special to her.

Follow-Up: There's a sequel to the book called *Skylark* that you can also read with your child.

The Chocolate Touch
Author: Patrick Skene Catling
Publisher: Morrow Junior Books

This is about a boy who loves chocolate. He eats a piece of chocolate that turns everything his lips touch to chocolate. He thinks it is wonderful at first, but he soon discovers differently.

Special Considerations: Your child should be able to read this book on his own.

Learning: Your child should learn from this book that having too much of something is not always a good thing.

Activity: Use a Venn, or web, diagram to compare the story to King Midas and the Golden Touch.

Follow-Up: Head to the kitchen and bake something chocolate.

Little House on the Prairie
Author: Laura Ingalls Wilder
Publisher: HarperTrophy

The Ingalls family moved from Wisconsin to Kansas and built their house on the prairie. Life on the farm can be difficult. This book describes what the family went through on a daily basis to survive. It also has adventures with cowboys, Indians, a panther, and even Santa Claus.

Special Considerations: This is a longer chapter book, so you may want to read it with your child.

Learning: Does your child want new things all the time? Is her holiday list always a mile long? This would be a great book to teach your child about life in the past when families and children didn't have a lot of possessions.

Activity: Use a Venn, or web, diagram to compare and contrast the similarities and differences between Laura's life and your child's life.

Follow-Up: You and your child could also read the other books in the series together. You could discuss the types of food available to Laura and her family compared to what families eat today. Which do you think is the best? Why?

B

SOFTWARE FOR THIRD GRADERS

Are you anxious to use your computer as a learning tool? I bet you told yourself that educational software is the real reason you needed to get the upgraded media package. Here is the chance to redeem youself. This appendix provides a list of software titles that are appropriate and interesting for third grade learners. Since your child may be more adept at the technical portion of the activity, it is not listed. If all else fails, refer to the software user's guide. You can find more recommended computer resources for your third grader at www .knowledgeessentials.com.

JumpStart Advanced 3rd Grade
Knowledge Adventure

JumpStart Advanced 3rd Grade has more fun and enriching learning activities than ever in its new mystery-themed three-CD set designed to prepare your child for third grade. This innovative educational software includes many great features. Auto leveling allows your child to learn at a pace that is just right for him.

Quantum Pad Library: 3rd Grade LeapPad Book: Science
Leapfrog

Dive into science with this fun, interactive science book for the Quantum Pad learning system. The book teaches concepts that students need to know to excel in third grade science and beyond. All science content was created to reflect state and national standards.

JumpStart 3rd Grade
Knowledge Adventure

Your child will need to draw on skills in reading, math, science, and music to stop time-meddling robots in this learning adventure. The difficulty level can be adjusted to match each student's ability. Automatically tracks students' progress.

School Zone Power Pack 3rd Grade
School Zone

Take kids on a fun journey through the world of third grade math—from fractions to multiplication and division. Game cards, flash cards, and puzzles will reinforce skills as kids play.

Cluefinders Math Adventures
Learning Tree

Build a bevy of sharp math skills as you trek high in the Himalayas with the Cluefinders. They're on a quest to find missing ancient treasures, and they need your sharp wits to hunt for clues. From purchasing supplies in the village store to building a yak corral, every activity is a math learning challenge. There are fifteen interactive learning games and exercises at ten different skill levels. Build more than twenty-five key math skills, including number computation, fractions and decimals, tables and graphs, and early geometry.

Schoolhouse Rock! 3rd & 4th Grade Deluxe
Creative Wonders

Schoolhouse Rock 3rd & 4th Grade Deluxe features two CD-ROMs packed with activities that develop important skills in math, grammar, language arts, geography, science, and history. As children explore the music and magic of Schoolhouse Rock, they will discover seventy activity combinations, original Schoolhouse Rock musical videos, plus dozens of printable games, puzzles, and experiments.

I Love Spelling
Global Software Publishing

Six exciting games make spelling fun! Start with a hilarious game-show format. Then mix in fast-action intergalactic games. Now you've got one surprising, fantastically fun way to learn the spelling of over five thousand commonly used English words.

U.S. Geography
Fogware Publishing

A ten-CD-ROM set that takes you on a spectacular journey across America, from the Atlantic to the Pacific coasts, then you venture on to Alaska and Hawaii. Cross mountains, deserts, plains, and forests as you visit all the states and major cities of each region.

View nature's greatest sculpture, the Grand Canyon, explore the wondrous scenery of Mount Hood, climb the giant redwoods, and marvel at Niagara Falls. The multisensory learning approach will appeal to students and ensure in-depth understanding and interest. This set features over four hundred minutes of multimedia content, sixty-eight hundred images that can be enlarged and printed, and a thousand interactive questions with automatic quizzes.

Cluefinders Reading Adventures
Learning Company

A two-CD-ROM set in which the Cluefinders are transported across the galaxy to rescue a dying planet from the grasp of the sorceress

Malicia. Travel from crystal caverns to mystic mountains to the top of Mount Valdrok. Explore and decipher suspicious objects. Investigate mysterious caverns to find the missing amulet. It's up to you and the Cluefinders to uncover the planet's secrets and collect useful clues to unlock the mystery. But beware—not all is as it appears!

3rd and 4th Grade Excelerator

TOPICS Entertainment

This two-CD-ROM set combines fun with proven educational principles to teach your child the fundamentals needed to excel in the third and fourth grades. Covering more than fifteen key topics, your child will grow with confidence as she masters the essential concepts of reading, creative writing, and mathematics.

C

THIRD GRADE TOPICAL CALENDAR

This calendar tells you approximately when the skills covered in this book occur during the school year. There will be variances, of course, but for the most part the skills build on one another, so it is logical that your child will learn things in a certain order.

Reading	Writing	Math	Science	Social Studies
September				
Compound words	Parts of speech	Place value	Measurement	Parts of a map
Parts of a story		Compare and order numbers	Reading charts, tables, and graphs	Landforms
		Patterns		
October				
Compound words	Sentence parts	Addition of up to two four-digit numbers	Classification	Prime meridian
Contractions	Grammar			Equator
Parts of a story	Cursive letters	Addition of three or more three-digit numbers		Map symbols
		Subtraction of up to two four-digit numbers		Landforms
		Estimating sums and differences		

Reading	Writing	Math	Science	Social Studies
November				
Compound words	Paragraphs	Basic multiplication facts	Systems	Using grids
Contractions	Grammar		Subsystems	Map symbols
Parts of a story	Cursive letters			Landforms
December				
Compound words	Paragraphs	Basic multiplication facts	Sound	Government
Contractions	Grammar			Holiday traditions
Parts of a story	Cursive letters			
January				
Synonyms	Paragraphs	Basic division facts	Life science	Government
Parts of a story	Grammar		Needs and character-	
	Cursive letters		istics of organisms	
February				
Homonyms	Book reports	Fractions	Habitats	Habitats
Parts of a story	Grammar			
	Connecting cursive letters			
March				
Synonyms	Book reports	Shapes and solids	Producers, herbi-	Economics
Homonyms	Grammar	Congruent figures	vores, and carnivores	
Parts of a story	Connecting cursive letters	Lines of symmetry	Food chain	
April				
Synonyms	Book reports	Coordinate graphing	Forces of nature:	Landforms
Homonyms	Grammar	Measurement	earthquakes, volcanoes, and	Economics
Parts of a story	Connecting cursive letters	Perimeter and area	glaciers	
May				
Parts of a story	Grammar	Collect, organize, and record information	How erosion changes the landscape	Landforms
	Connecting curive letters	Basic probability		Economics
		Permutations		

GLOSSARY

accountability   Holding students responsible for what they learn and teachers responsible for what they teach.

achievement test   A test designed to efficiently measure the amount of knowledge and/or skill a person has acquired. This helps evaluate student learning in comparison with a standard or norm.

adjective   A word that modifies a noun. It describes a quality of a person, place, or thing.

adverb   A word that describes a verb, adjective, or another adverb. It often ends in "ly."

antonym   A word that has an opposite meaning of another word.

area   A measure of a surface with boundaries—for example, a square or a triangle. Area is measured in square units.

assessment   Measuring a student's learning.

authentic assessment   The concept of model, practice, and feedback in which students know what excellent performance is and are guided to practice an entire concept rather than bits and pieces in preparation for eventual understanding.

bay   A body of water that is a part of a sea or an ocean. It is partly enclosed by land.

benchmark   A standard by which student performance can be measured in order to compare it with and improve one's own skills or learning.

Bloom's taxonomy   A classification system for learning objectives that consists of six levels ranging from knowledge (which focuses on the reproduction of facts) to evaluation (which represents higher-level thinking).

bluff   The high, steep side of a rock or the earth.

canyon   A deep, narrow valley with steep sides.

cardinal directions   The four main directions: north, south, east, and west.

cartographer   A person who makes maps.

cliff   The high, steep side of a rock or the earth.

coast   Land along a sea or an ocean.

compass rose   A symbol on a map that shows the directions.

competency test   A test intended to determine whether a student has met established minimum standards of skills and knowledge and is thus eligible for promotion, graduation, certification, or other official acknowledgment of achievement.

comprehension   The understanding of what you have read.

concept   An abstract, general notion—a heading that characterizes a set of behaviors and beliefs.

cone   A three-dimensional shape that has a circle for a base, a curved surface, and comes to a point at the top.

congruent   Shapes that have the same size and shape.

conjunction   A word such as "and," "or," and "but" that connects other words, ideas, phrases, clauses, and sentences.

content goals   Statements that are like learning standards or learning objectives, but which only describe the topics to be studied, not the skills to be performed.

contraction   A word or a phrase that is formed by leaving out one or more letters or combining some of the sounds of a longer phrase.

coordinate graph   A device for locating points in a plane by using ordered pairs of numbers. The graph is formed by the intersection of two number lines. The intersection forms right angles.

criterion-referenced test   A test in which the results can be used to determine a student's progress toward mastery of a content area or designated objectives of an instructional program. Performance is compared to an expected level of mastery in a content area rather than to other students' scores.

cube   A three-dimensional shape with six square faces.

curriculum The content and skills that are taught at each grade level.

curriculum alignment The connection of subjects across grade levels, cumulatively, to build comprehensive, increasingly complex instructional programs.

cylinder A three-dimensional shape that has a curved surface and parallel, congruent, circular, or elliptical bases.

denominator The bottom number of a fraction. It represents the number of equal parts in which the object has been broken.

desert An area of dry land without many plants.

developmental delay Occurs when a child is developing skills that only come with emotional and intellectual growth more slowly than other students who are his same age, but he is developing those skills properly. There is no reason to believe there is a problem that time can't solve.

developmental disorder Occurs when a child is developing skills that only come with emotional and intellectual growth more slowly than other students who are her same age, or she is not developing those developmental skills at all or not in a normal way. She may have a problem that can be solved.

direct object A noun or pronoun that is having an action done to it.

dividend The number that is being divided in a division problem.

divisor The number that divides another number in a division problem.

elapsed time The amount of time that has passed while some event is happening.

elevation The height of the land.

equator An imaginary line that divides the earth into the northern hemisphere and the southern hemisphere.

equivalent Having the same value.

erosion Occurs when material is being worn away from the earth's surface by weathering.

estimate An approximate amount or value.

fact families   Show how addition and subtraction as well as multiplication and division are related.

fluency   The ability to read quickly and effortlessly.

genre   A type of literary work.

graphic organizer   An aid to organize information in order to remember and understand the information.

gulf   A large body of water that is partly enclosed by land.

habitat   The place where an organism usually lives.

harbor   An area of water where ships can dock.

hemisphere   Either the northern or southern half of the earth as divided by the equator or the eastern or western half of the earth as divided by the prime meridian.

high-stakes testing   Any testing program whose results have important consequences for students, teachers, colleges, and/or areas, such as promotion, certification, graduation, or denial/approval of services and opportunity.

hill   Land that is taller than the land around it.

homonyms   Words that sound the same but have different meanings. The words can be spelled the same or have different spellings.

indirect object   A noun or pronoun that tells you for what or whom the action of the verb (predicate) is being done.

interjection   An exclamation or utterance, such as "wow," "oh," or "huh."

intermediate directions   The directions between the cardinal directions. They are northeast, northwest, southeast, and southwest.

IQ test   A psychometric test that scores the performance of certain intellectual tasks and can provide assessors with a measurement of general intelligence.

island   Land that is completely surrounded by water.

lake   A body of water that is surrounded by land.

learning disability   Occurs when a child is not able to learn in the same way or at the same pace at which other students his own age learn. Developmental skills needed at this age are either missing or hyperdeveloped.

learning objectives   A set of expectations that are needed to meet the learning standard.

learning standards   Broad statements that describe what content a student should know and what skills a student should be able to demonstrate in different subject areas.

mass   The physical volume of a solid body.

measurement   Quantitative description of student learning and qualitative description of student attitude.

median   The point on a scale that divides a group into two equal subgroups. The median is not affected by low or high scores as is the mean. (See also **norm**.)

metacognition   The knowledge of one's own thinking processes and strategies, and the ability to consciously reflect and act on the knowledge of cognition to modify those processes and strategies.

mountain   The tallest type of landform.

multiple-choice test   A test in which students are presented with a question or an incomplete sentence or idea. The students are expected to choose the correct or best answer or completion from a menu of alternatives.

norm   A distribution of scores obtained from a norm group. The norm is the midpoint (or median) of scores or performance of the students in that group. Fifty percent will score above the norm and 50 percent will score below it.

norm group   A random group of students selected by a test developer to take a test to provide a range of scores and establish the percentiles of performance for use in determining scoring standards.

norm-referenced test   A test in which a student or a group's performance is compared to that of a norm group. The results are relative to the performance of an external group and are designed to be compared with the norm group, resulting in a performance standard. These tests are often used to measure and compare students, schools, districts, and states on the basis of norm-established scales of achievement.

noun   A word that names a person, place, thing, feeling, idea, or act.

ocean   A large body of salt water.

organism   An individual form of life, such as a plant or an animal.

outcome   An operationally defined educational goal, usually a culminating activity, product, or performance that can be measured.

peninsula   Land that is almost completely surrounded by water.

performance-based assessment   Direct observation and rating of student performance of an educational objective, often an ongoing observation over a period of time, and typically involving the creation of products dealing with real life. Performance-based assessments use performance criteria to determine the degree to which a student has met an achievement target. Important elements of performance-based assessment include clear goals or performance criteria clearly articulated and communicated to the learner.

performance goals   Statements that are like learning standards or learning objectives, but they only describe the skills to be performed, not the content to be studied.

perimeter   The distance around a closed figure.

permutations   The changing of the elements in a set.

place value   The value of a digit as determined by its position in a number.

plain   A large area of flat land.

plateau   An area of high flat land with steep sides.

plural noun   A noun that refers to two or more people, places, or things.

portfolio assessment   A systematic and organized collection of a student's work that exhibits to others the direct evidence of a student's efforts, achievements, and progress over a period of time. The collection should involve the student in selection of its contents and should include information about the performance criteria, the rubric or criteria for judging merit, and evidence of student self-relocation or evaluation. It should include representative work, providing documentation of the learner's performance and a basis for evaluation of the student's progress. Portfolios may include a variety of demonstrations of learning.

predicate   A verb that describes what the noun (subject) of a sentence is doing or being.

preposition   A word that shows the relationship between one noun and a different noun, verb, or adverb, such as "in" or "through."

prime meridian   An imaginary line that divides the earth into the eastern hemisphere and the western hemisphere.

probability   A number from 0 to 1 that shows the likelihood that an event will happen.

product   The answer you get when you multiply numbers.

product map   A map that shows the various products that are in a state or region.

pronoun   A word that replaces a noun, such as "he," "they," or "it."

proper noun   The name of a particular person (someone's name), place, or thing; it begins with a capital letter.

pyramid   A three-dimensional shape in which the base is some type of polygon and all of the sides are triangles.

rectangular prism   A prism whose faces, including the bases, are all rectangles.

regrouping   A process used in subtraction. You might have to regroup from one place value position to another in order to have enough to subtract from each place value position. For example, you might need to take 10 from the tens position and regroup it as ten ones in the ones position.

river   A large stream of water that flows across the land.

rounding   A type of estimation. For example, if you round 230 to the nearest hundred, you ask yourself if the number is closer to 200 or 300. The answer is 200.

scientific method   The principles and procedures of discovery and demonstration that are necessary for a scientific experiment.

sea   A body of salt water that is smaller than an ocean.

shore   The land along the edge of an ocean, sea, lake, or river.

singular noun   A noun that refers to one person, place, or thing.

solid   Having a definite shape and volume.

sphere   A three-dimensional shape with a curved surface that is at all points a given distance from its center point. A ball is an example of a sphere.

statistics   A number value such as the mean that characterizes the sample from which it came.

strait   A narrow channel of water that connects two larger bodies of water.

subject   A noun or pronoun that is performing the verb; the "do-er" of a sentence.

subsystem   A part of a larger system that works together to make the whole system work.

sum   The answer you get when you add.

summary   A compilation of the main ideas or events.

swamp   An area of low, wet land with trees.

symmetry   When an object or shape is divided in half, both sides are exactly the same.

synonym   A word that means the same as another word.

system   A group of interacting elements that form a whole.

topographic map   A map with detailed and raised areas that show the shape of the surface of the land.

tributary   A stream or river that empties into a larger river.

valley   An area of low land between hills or mountains.

verb   A word that describes action.

verb tense   The "tense" of a verb tells you when the action happened. The main forms are present (I sing), past (I sung), future (I will sing), present participle (I am singing), and past participle (I have sung).

volcano   An opening in the earth through which lava, rock, ashes, and gases are forced out.

BIBLIOGRAPHY

Bloom, B. S. (ed.) (1956). *Taxonomy of Educational Objectives: The Classification of Educational Goals: Handbook I, Cognitive Domain.* New York: Longmans, Green.

Brainerd, C. J. (1978). *Piaget's Theory of Intelligence.* New Jersey: Prentice Hall, Inc.

Evans, R. (1973). *Jean Piaget: The Man and His Ideas.* New York: E. P. Dutton & Co., Inc.

Lavatelli, C. (1973). *Piaget's Theory Applied to an Early Childhood Curriculum.* Boston: American Science and Engineering, Inc.

London, C. (1988). "A Piagetian constructivist perspective on curriculum development." *Reading Improvement 27,* 82–95.

Piaget, J. (1972). "Development and Learning." In Lavatelli, C. S., and Stendler, F. *Reading in Child Behavior and Development.* New York: Harcourt Brace Janovich.

——— (1972). *To Understand Is to Invent.* New York: The Viking Press, Inc.

Shure, M. B. (1993). *Interpersonal Problem Solving and Prevention: A Comprehensive Report of Research and Training.* A five-year longitudinal study, Kindergarten through grade 4, no. MH-40801. Washington, D.C.: National Institute of Mental Health.

Shure, M. B., and G. Spivack (1980). "Interpersonal Problem Solving as a Mediator of Behavioral Adjustment in Preschool and Kindergarten Children." *Journal of Applied Developmental Psychology 1* 29–44.

——— (1982). "Interpersonal Problem-solving in Young Children: A Cognitive Approach to Prevention." *American Journal of Community Psychology 10,* 341–356.

Sigel, I., and R. Cocking (1977). *Cognitive Development from Childhood to Adolescence: A Constructivist Perspective.* New York: Holt, Rinehart and Winston.

Singer, D., and T. Revenson (1978). *A Piaget Primer: How a Child Thinks.* New York: International Universities Press, Inc.

Willis, Mariaemma, and Victoria Hodson (1999). *Discover Your Child's Learning Style.* New York: Crown Publishing Group.

INDEX